THE NATURE OF ARIZONA

AN INTRODUCTION TO FAMILIAR
PLANTS, ANIMALS & OUTSTANDING
NATURAL ATTRACTIONS

WATERFORD PRESS

Reviews for the companion guide, *The Nature of California*:

"The Nature of California offers an agreeable overview of animals and plants casual hikers and campers are likely to encounter . . . a useful book to keep with the picnic supplies or camping gear."

Los Angeles Times

"With so many detailed guides in print, it would be tempting to overlook this book, yet it fills a valuable niche. Small and light, [it features] lovely color illustrations of several hundred species of plants, mammals, reptiles, fish and birds."

San Francisco Chronicle

"A useful and informative guide . . . this is a user-friendly book with an excellent introduction."

Books of the Southwest Review

"A colorful paperback field guide for people of all ages."

California Biodiversity News

THE
NATURE
OF
ARIZONA

AN INTRODUCTION TO FAMILIAR PLANTS, ANIMALS & OUTSTANDING NATURAL ATTRACTIONS

By James Kavanagh

Illustrations by Raymond Leung

Introduction by James C. Rettie

WATERFORD PRESS

Publisher's Cataloging in Publication Data
Kavanagh, James Daniel, 1960-
The Nature of Arizona. An Introduction to Familiar Plants, Animals & Outstanding Natural Attractions (2nd ed). Includes bibliographical references, checklists and index.
1. Natural History – Arizona. 2. Animals – Identification – Arizona.
3. Plants – Identification – Arizona. 4. Tourism – Arizona.

Library of Congress Catalog Card Number: 2005936117
ISBN 10: 1-58355-300-2
ISBN 13: 978-1-58355-300-8

The introductory essay, "BUT A WATCH IN THE NIGHT" by JAMES C. RETTIE is from FOREVER THE LAND by RUSSELL AND KATE LORD. Copyright © 1950 by Harper & Brothers, copyright renewed © 1978 by Russell and Kate Lord. Reprinted with permission of HarperCollins Publishers.

The publisher would like to acknowledge the following institutions and individuals who assisted in the research and production of this guide:
Arizona State Parks Board
Arizona Department of Tourism
The Phoenix Zoo, Education Department
The Desert Botanical Garden, Phoenix
Coconino and Prescott National Forests
The U.S. Fish & Wildlife Service
The Arizona-Sonora Desert Museum, Education Department
Roseann Beggy Hanson   Jonathan Hanson
Matt Chu   Peter Haibeck
Bill Silvey   Karen Schedler
Sonya Nevin

Waterford Press' toll-free order/information line is (800) 434-2555.
Download hundreds of educational activities and games from our website:
www.waterfordpress.com

While every attempt has been made to ensure the accuracy of the information in this guide, it is important to note that experts often disagree with one another regarding the common name, size, appearance, habitat, distribution and taxonomy of species. For permissions, or to share comments, e-mail editor@waterfordpress.com.

Printed in China

CONTENTS

To Kristen

PREFACE

The Nature of Arizona is intended to provide novice naturalists with a simplified pocket reference to familiar and distinctive species of plants and animals and the outstanding natural attractions found in Arizona.

The guide's primary purpose is to introduce the reader to plants and animals and highlight the diversity of species found in Arizona. Its secondary purpose is to show how all species in each ecosystem found here – from deserts to alpine forests – depend on each other, directly and indirectly, for survival.

Environmental education begins when individuals learn to appreciate the plants and animals in their immediate environment. When they start to care about local species – which often begins by learning their names – they take the first step toward understanding their place (as an animal) within an ecosystem.

The guide opens with a brief introduction to evolution. This is not intended in any way to dispute creationism, but is merely intended to illustrate the similarities and differences between major groups of plants and animals and show when each appeared in geologic time. To study the fossil record is fascinating in and of itself, but one of the most stunning things it reveals is a number of transitional species that are intermediary between different classes of organisms.

The brilliant introductory essay by James C. Rettie provides a simplified view of the evolution of life on earth, and the role that man – the animal – has played to date.

J.D.K.

BUT A WATCH IN THE NIGHT

BY JAMES C. RETTIE

James C. Rettie wrote the following essay while working for the National Forest Service in 1948. In a flash of brilliance, he converted the statistics from an existing government pamphlet on soil erosion into an analogy for the ages.

OUT BEYOND OUR SOLAR SYSTEM there is a planet called Copernicus. It came into existence some four or five billion years before the birth of our earth. In due course of time it became inhabited by a race of intelligent men.

About 750 million years ago the Copernicans had developed the motion picture machine to a point well in advance of the stage that we have reached. Most of the cameras that we now use in motion picture work are geared to take twenty-four pictures per second on a continuous strip of film. When such film is run through a projector, it throws a series of images on the screen and these change with a rapidity that gives the visual impression of normal movement. If a motion is too swift for the human eye to see it in detail, it can be captured and artificially slowed down by means of the slow-motion camera. This one is geared to take many more shots per second – ninety-six or even more than that. When the slow motion film is projected at the normal speed of twenty-four pictures per second, we can see just how the jumping horse goes over a hurdle.

What about motion that is too slow to be seen by the human eye? That problem has been solved by the use of the time-lapse camera. In this one, the shutter is geared to take only one shot per second, or one per minute, or even one per hour – depending upon the kind of movement that is being photographed. When the time-lapse film is projected at the normal speed of twenty-four pictures per second, it is possible to see a bean sprout growing up out of the ground. Time-lapse films are useful in the study of many types of motion too slow to be observed by the unaided, human eye.

The Copernicans, it seems, had time-lapse cameras some 757 million years ago and they also had superpowered telescopes that gave them a clear view of what was happening upon this earth. They decided to make a film record of the life history of earth and to make it on the scale of one picture per year. The photography has been in progress during the last 757 million years.

In the near future, a Copernican interstellar expedition will arrive upon our earth and bring with it a copy of the time-lapse film. Arrangements will be made for showing the entire film in one continuous run. This will begin at midnight of New Year's eve and continue day and night without a single stop until midnight on December 31. The rate of projection will be 24 pictures per second. Time on the screen will thus seem to move at the rate of twenty-four years per second; 1440 years per minute; 86,400 years per hour; approximately two million years per day and sixty-two million years per month. The normal lifespan of individual man will occupy about three seconds. The full period of earth history that will be unfolded on the screen (some 757 million years) will extend from what the geologists call the Pre-Cambrian times up to the present. This will, by no means, cover the full time-span of the earth's geological history but it will embrace the period since the advent of living organisms.

During the months of January, February, and March the picture will be desolate and dreary. The shape of the land masses and the oceans will bear little or no resemblance to those that we know. The violence of geological erosion will be much in evidence. Rains will pour down on the land and promptly go booming down to the seas. There will be no clear streams anywhere except where the rains fall upon hard rock. Everywhere on the steeper ground the stream channels will be filled with boulders hurled down by rushing waters. Raging torrents and dry stream beds will keep alternating in quick succession. High mountains will seem to melt like so much butter in the sun. The shifting of land into the seas, later to be thrust up as new mountains, will be going on at a grand scale.

Early in April there will be some indication of the presence of single-celled living organisms in some of the warmer and sheltered coastal waters. By the end of the month it will be noticed that some of these organisms have become multicellular. A few of them, including the Trilobites, will be encased in hard shells.

Toward the end of May, the first vertebrates will appear, but they will still be aquatic creatures. In June about 60 percent of the land area that we know as North America will be under water. One broad channel will occupy the space where the Rocky Mountains now stand. Great deposits of limestone will be forming under some of the shallower seas. Oil and gas deposits will be in process of formation – also under shallow seas. On land there will be no sign of vegetation. Erosion will be rampant, tearing loose particles and chunks of rock and grinding them into sand and silt to be spewed out by the streams into bays and estuaries.

About the middle of July the first land plants will appear and take up the tremendous job of soil building. Slowly, very slowly, the mat of vegetation will spread, always battling for its life against the power of erosion. Almost foot by foot, the plant life will advance, lacing down with its root structures whatever pulverized rock material it can find. Leaves and stems will be giving added protection against the loss of the soil foothold. The increasing vegetation will pave the way for the land animals that will live upon it.

Early in August the seas will be teeming with fish. This will be what geologists call the Devonian period. Some of the races of these fish will be breathing by means of lung tissue instead of through gill tissues. Before the month is over, some of the lung fish will go ashore and take on a crude lizard-like appearance. Here are the first amphibians.

In early September the insects will put in their appearance. Some will look like huge dragonflies and will have a wing span of 24 inches. Large portions of the land masses will now be covered with heavy vegetation that will include the primitive spore-propagating trees. Layer upon layer of this plant growth will build up, later to appear as coal deposits. About the middle of this month, there will be evidence of the first seed-bearing plants and the first reptiles. Heretofore, the land animals will have been amphibians that could reproduce their kind only by depositing a soft egg mass in quiet waters. The reptiles will be shown to be freed from the aquatic bond because they can reproduce by means of a shelled egg in which the embryo and its nurturing liquids are sealed and thus protected from destructive evaporation. Before September is over, the first dinosaurs will be seen – creatures destined to dominate the animal realm for about 140 million years and then to disappear.

In October there will be series of mountain uplifts along what is now the eastern coast of the United States. A creature with feathered limbs – half bird and half reptile in appearance – will take itself into the air. Some small and rather unpretentious animals will be seen to bring forth their young in a form that is a miniature replica of the parents and to feed these young on milk secreted by mammary glands in the female parent. The emergence of this mammalian form of animal life will be recognized as one of the great events in geologic time. October will also witness the high-water mark of the dinosaurs – creatures ranging in size from that of the modern goat to monsters like Brontosaurus that weighed some 40 tons. Most of them will be placid vegetarians, but a few will be hideous-looking carnivores, like Allosaurus and Tyrannosaurus. Some of the herbivorous dinosaurs will be clad in bony armor for protection against their flesh-eating comrades.

November will bring pictures of a sea extending from the Gulf of Mexico to the Arctic in space now occupied by the Rocky Mountains. A few of the reptiles will take to the air on bat-like wings. One of these, called Pteranodon, will have a wingspread of 15 feet. There will be a rapid development of the modern flowering plants, modern trees, and modern insects. The dinosaurs will disappear. Toward the end of the month there will be a tremendous land disturbance in which the Rocky Mountains will rise out of the sea to assume a dominating place in the North American landscape.

As the picture runs on into December it will show the mammals in command of the animal life. Seed-bearing trees and grasses will have covered most of the land with a heavy mantle of vegetation. Only the areas newly thrust up from the sea will be barren. Most of the streams will be crystal clear. The turmoil of geological erosion will be confined to localized areas. About December 25 will begin the cutting of the Grand Canyon of the Colorado River. Grinding down through layer after layer of sedimentary strata, this stream will finally expose deposits laid down in Pre-Cambrian times. Thus in the walls of that canyon will appear geological formations dating from recent times to the period when the earth had no living organisms upon it.

The picture will run on through the latter days of December and even up to its final day with still no sign of mankind. The spectators will become alarmed in the fear that man has somehow been left out. But not so; sometime about noon on December 31 (one million years ago) will appear a stooped, massive creature of man-like proportions. This will be Pithecanthropus, the Java ape man. For tools and weapons he will have nothing but crude stone and wooden clubs. His children will live a precarious existence threatened on the one side by hostile animals and on the other by tremendous climatic changes. Ice sheets – in places 4,000 feet deep – will form in the northern parts of North America and Eurasia. Four times this glacial ice will push southward to cover half the continents. With each advance the plant and animal life will be swept under or pushed southward. With each recession of the ice, life will struggle to re-establish itself in the wake of the retreating glaciers. The woolly mammoth, the musk ox, and the caribou all will fight to maintain themselves near the ice line. Sometimes they will be caught and put into cold storage – skin, flesh, blood, bones, and all.

The picture will run on through supper time with still very little evidence of man's presence on earth. It will be about 11 o'clock when Neanderthal man appears. Another half hour will go by before the appearance of Cro-Magnon man living in caves and painting crude animal pictures on the walls of his dwelling. Fifteen minutes more will bring Neolithic man, knowing how to chip stone and thus produce sharp cutting edges for spears and tools. In a few minutes more it will appear that man has domesticated the dog, the sheep and, possibly, other animals. He will then begin the use of milk. He will also learn the arts of basket weaving and the making of pottery and dugout canoes.

The dawn of civilization will not come until about five or six minutes before the end of the picture. The story of the Egyptians, the Babylonians, the Greeks, and the Romans will unroll during the fourth, the third, and the second minute before the end. At 58 minutes and 43 seconds past 11:00 P.M. (just 1 minute and 17 seconds before the end) will come the beginning of the Christian era. Columbus will discover the new world 20 seconds before the end.

The Declaration of Independence will be signed just 7 seconds before the final curtain comes down.

In those few moments of geologic time will be the story of all that has happened since we became a nation. And what a story it will be! A human swarm will sweep across the face of the continent and take it away from the [Native Americans]. They will change it far more radically than it has ever been changed before in a comparable time. The great virgin forests will be seen going down before ax and fire. The soil, covered for eons by its protective mantle of trees and grasses, will be laid bare to the ravages of water and wind erosion. Streams that had been flowing clear will, once again, take up a load of silt and push it toward the seas. Humus and mineral salts, both vital elements of productive soil, will be seen to vanish at a terrifying rate.

The railroads and highways and cities that will spring up may divert attention, but they cannot cover up the blight of man's recent activities. In great sections of Asia, it will be seen that man must utilize cow dung and every scrap of available straw or grass for fuel to cook his food. The forests that once provided wood for this purpose will be gone without a trace. The use of these agricultural wastes for fuel, in place of returning them to the land, will be leading to increasing soil impoverishment. Here and there will be seen a dust storm darkening the landscape over an area a thousand miles across. Man-creatures will be shown counting their wealth in terms of bits of printed paper representing other bits of a scarce but comparatively useless yellow metal that is kept buried in strong vaults. Meanwhile, the soil, the only real wealth that can keep mankind alive on the face of this earth is savagely being cut loose from its ancient moorings and washed into the seven seas.

We have just arrived upon this earth. How long will we stay?

Because this guide has been written for the novice, every attempt has been made to simplify presentation of the material. Illustrations are accompanied by brief descriptions of key features, and technical terms have been held to a minimum. Plants and animals are arranged more-or-less in their taxonomic groupings. Exceptions have been made when nontraditional groupings facilitate field identification for the novice (e.g., wildflowers are grouped by color).

SPECIES DESCRIPTION

The species descriptions have been fragmented to simplify presentation of information:

① **ANNA'S HUMMINGBIRD**
② *Calypte anna*
③ **Size:** 3-4 in. (8-10 cm)
④ **Description:** Small, metallic-green bird. Male has red throat and head. Female has spotted throat.
⑤ **Habitat:** Urban areas, wooded canyons to middle elevations.
⑥ **Comments:** Subsists on a diet of nectar, insects and spiders. Many desert plants rely on hummingbirds for pollination.

① **COMMON NAME**

The name in bold type indicates the common name of the species. It is important to note that a single species may have many common names.

② *Scientific Name*

The italicized latin words refer to an organism's scientific name, a universally accepted two-part term that precisely defines its relationship to other organisms. The first capitalized word, the genus, refers to groups of closely related organisms. The second term, the species name, refers to organisms that look similar and interbreed freely. If the second word in the term is 'spp.', this indicates there are several species in the genus that look similar to the one illustrated. If a third word appears in the term, it identifies a subspecies, a group of individuals that are even more closely related.

③ Size

Generally indicates the maximum length of animals (nose to tail tip) and the maximum height of plants. Exceptions are noted in the text.

④ **Description**
Refers to key markings and/or characteristics that help to distinguish a species.

⑤ **Habitat**
Where a species lives/can be found.

⑥ **Comments**
General information regarding distinctive behaviors, diet, vocalizations, related species, etc.

ILLUSTRATIONS

The majority of animal illustrations show the adult male in its breeding coloration. Plant illustrations are designed to highlight the characteristics that are most conspicuous in the field. It is important to note that illustrations are merely meant as guidelines; coloration, size and shape will vary depending on age, sex or season.

SPECIES CHECKLISTS

The species checklists at the back of this book are provided to allow you to keep track of the plants and animals you identify.

TIPS ON FIELD IDENTIFICATION

Identifying a species in the field can be as simple as one, two, three:

1. Note key markings, characteristics and/or behaviors;
2. Find an illustration that matches; and
3. Read the text to confirm your sighting.

Identifying mammals or birds in the field is not fundamentally different than identifying trees, flowers or other forms of life. It is simply a matter of knowing what to look for. Reading the introductory text to each section will make you aware of key characteristics of each group and allow you to use the guide more effectively in the field.

N.B. – *We refer primarily to familiar species in this guide and do not list all species within any group. References listed in the bibliography at the back of this guide provide more detailed information about specific areas of study.*

EVOLUTION OF ANIMALS

WHAT IS AN ANIMAL?

Animals are living organisms which can generally be distinguished from plants in four ways:
1) They feed on plants and other animals;
2) They have a nervous system;
3) They can move freely and are not rooted; and
4) Their cells do not have rigid walls or contain chlorophyll.

All animals are members of the animal kingdom, a group consisting of more than a million species. Species are classified within the animal kingdom according to their evolutionary relationships to one another.

Most of the animals discussed in this guide are members of the group called vertebrates. They all possess backbones and most have complex brains and highly developed senses.

The earliest vertebrates appeared in the oceans about 500 million years ago. Today, surviving species are divided into five main groups.

1. Fishes
2. Amphibians
3. Reptiles
4. Birds
5. Mammals

Following is a simplified description of the evolution of the vertebrates and the differences between groups.

FISHES

The oldest form of vertebrate life, fishes evolved from invertebrate sea creatures 400-500 million years ago. All are cold-blooded (ectothermic) and their activity levels are largely influenced by the surrounding environment.

The first species were armored and jawless and fed by filtering tiny organisms from water and mud. Surviving members of this group include lampreys and hagfishes. Jawless fishes were succeeded by jawed fishes that quickly came to dominate the seas, and still do today. The major surviving groups include:

1) **Sharks and rays** – more primitive species that possess soft skeletons made of cartilage; and

2) **Bony fishes** – a more advanced group of fishes that have bony skeletons, it includes most of the fishes currently existing.

Shark

Ray

Bony Fish

Physiological Characteristics of Fishes

Heart and gills
A two-chambered heart circulates the blood through a simple system of arteries and veins. Gills act like lungs and allow fishes to absorb dissolved oxygen from the water into their bloodstream.

Nervous system
Small anterior brain is connected to a spinal cord which runs the length of the body.

Digestive system
Digestive system is complete. A number of specialized organs produce enzymes which help to break down food in the stomach and intestines. Kidneys extract urine from the blood and waste is eliminated through the anus.

Reproduction
In most fishes, the female lays numerous eggs in water and the male fertilizes them externally. Young usually hatch as larvae, and the larval period ranges from a few hours to several years. Survival rate of young is low.

Senses
Most have the senses of taste, touch, smell, hearing and sight, although their vision is generally poor. Fishes hear and feel by sensing vibrations and temperature and pressure changes in the surrounding water.

AMPHIBIANS

The first limbed land-dwellers, amphibians evolved from fishes 300-400 million years ago and became the dominant land vertebrates for more than 100 million years. Like fishes, amphibians are cold-blooded and their activity levels are largely influenced by the environment.

The first fish-like amphibian ancestors to escape the water were those that had the ability to breathe air and possessed strong, paired fins that allowed them to wriggle onto mud-flats and sandbars. (Living relics of this group include five species of lungfish and the rare coelacanth.) Although amphibians were able to exploit rich new habitats on land, they remained largely dependent on aquatic environments for survival and reproduction.

The major surviving groups are:

1) **Salamanders** – slender-bodied, short-legged, long-tailed creatures that live secretive lives in dark, damp areas; and

2) **Frogs and toads** – squat-bodied animals with long hind legs, large heads and large eyes. Frogs are smooth skinned, toads have warty skin.

Salamander

Frog

Toad

Advances Made Over Fishes

Lungs and legs
By developing lungs and legs, amphibians freed themselves from the competition for food in aquatic environments and were able to flourish on land.

Improved circulatory system
Amphibians evolved a heart with three chambers that enhanced gas exchange in the lungs and provided body tissues with highly oxygenated blood.

Ears
Frogs and toads developed external ears that enhanced their hearing ability, an essential adaptation for surviving on land.

Reproduction
Most amphibians reproduced like fish. Salamanders differ in that most fertilize eggs internally rather than externally. In many, the male produced a sperm packet which the female collected and used to fertilize eggs as they were laid.

REPTILES

Reptiles appeared 300-350 million years ago. They soon came to dominate the earth, and continued to rule the land, sea and air for more than 130 million years. Cold-blooded like amphibians, reptiles evolved a host of characteristics that made them better suited for life on land.

About 65 million years ago, the dominant reptiles mysteriously underwent a mass extinction. A popular theory suggests this was caused by a giant meteor hitting the earth which sent up a huge dust cloud that blotted out the sun. The lack of sun and subsequently low temperatures caused many plants and animals to perish.

The major surviving reptilian groups are:

1) **Turtles** – hard-shelled reptiles with short legs;
2) **Lizards** – scaly-skinned reptiles with long legs and tails;
3) **Snakes** – long, legless reptiles with scaly skin; and
4) **Crocodilians** – very large reptiles with elongate snouts, toothy jaws and long tails.

Lizards
(skinks, geckos, iguanas, etc.)

Snakes
(rattlesnakes, garter snakes, constrictors, etc.)

Turtles
(turtles, sea turtles and tortoises)

Crocodilians
(alligators and crocodiles)

Advances Made Over Amphibians

Dry, scaly skin
Their dry skin prevents water loss and also protects them from predators.

Posture
Many reptiles evolved an upright posture and strong legs which enhanced their mobility on land.

Improved heart and lungs
Their heart and lungs were more efficient which heightened their activity levels. The heart had four chambers – although the division between ventricles was usually incomplete – making it less likely that oxygenated and deoxygenated blood would mix.

Defense
They were agile and better able to defend themselves, having sharp claws and teeth or beaks capable of inflicting wounds.

BIRDS

Birds evolved from reptiles 100-200 million years ago. Unlike species before them, birds were warm-blooded (endothermic) and able to regulate their body temperature internally.* This meant that they could maintain high activity levels despite fluctuations in environmental temperature. They are believed to have evolved from a group of gliding reptiles, with their scaly legs considered proof of their reptilian heritage.

Birds come in a vast array of groups. All have feathered bodies, beaks, lack teeth and have forelimbs modified into wings. Most can fly.

Advances Made Over Reptiles

Ability to fly
By evolving flight, birds were able to exploit environments that were inaccessible to their competitors and predators. The characteristics they evolved that allowed them to fly included wings, feathers, hollow bones and an enhanced breathing capacity.

Warm-blooded
An insulating layer of feathers enhanced their capacity to retain heat. They also had true four-chambered hearts that enhanced their ability to maintain high activity levels in varying environments.

Keen senses
Birds evolved very keen senses of vision and hearing and developed complex behavioral and communicative patterns.

Reproduction
Fertilization was internal and the eggs had hard, rather than leathery, shells. Unlike most reptiles, birds incubated their eggs themselves and protected and nurtured their young for a period of time following birth.

* There is still a debate over whether or not some dinosaurs were warm-blooded.

MAMMALS

Mammals evolved from reptiles 100-200 million years ago. Though warm-blooded like birds, they are believed to have different reptilian ancestors. In addition to being warm-blooded, mammals also evolved physiological adaptations which allowed them to hunt prey and avoid predation better than their competitors.

Mammals quickly exploited the habitats left vacant by the dinosaurs and have been the dominant land vertebrates for the past 65 million years. Man is a relatively new addition to the group, having a lineage of less than 3 million years.

Mammals have evolved into three distinct groups, all of which have living representatives:

1) **Monotremes** – egg-laying mammals;
2) **Marsupials** – pouched mammals which bear living, embryonic young; and
3) **Placentals** – mammals which bear fully-developed young.

Monotremes
(platypus and echidna)

Marsupials
(opossums,
kangaroos etc.)

Placentals
(squirrels, humans,
dogs, rats etc.)

Advances Made Over Birds

Reproduction
Fertilization was internal, but in most, the young developed in the female's uterus instead of an egg. After birth, the young were fed and nurtured by adults for an extensive period, during which they learned behavioral lessons from their elders and siblings. This emphasis on learned responses at an early age is believed to contributed to the superior intelligence and reproductive success of the group.

Hearing
Most had three bones in the middle ear to enhance hearing. (Birds and reptiles have one.)

Teeth
Many developed specialized teeth that allowed them to rely on a variety of food sources. Incisors were for cutting, canines for tearing and molars for chewing or shearing.

Breathing
Mammals evolved a diaphragm which increased breathing efficiency.

Posture
Many evolved long, strong legs and were very agile on land.

EVOLUTION OF PLANTS

WHAT IS A PLANT?

Plants are living organisms which can generally be distinguished from animals in four ways:

1) They synthesize their own food needed for maintenance and growth from carbon dioxide, water and sunlight;
2) They do not have a nervous system;
3) Most are rooted and cannot move around easily; and
4) Their cells have rigid walls and contain chlorophyll, a pigment needed for photosynthesis.

All plants are members of the plant kingdom. According to the fossil record, plants evolved from algae that originated nearly 3 billion years ago. Since then, plants have evolved into millions of species in a mind-boggling assortment of groups.

Most North American plants are classified into two main groups:

1) **Gymnosperms** – plants with naked seeds; and
2) **Angiosperms** – flowering plants with enclosed seeds.

Gymnosperms   Angiosperms

GYMNOSPERMS – THE NAKED SEED PLANTS

This group of mostly evergreen trees and shrubs includes some of the largest and oldest known plants. They began to appear around 300-400 million years ago, and were the dominant plant species on earth for nearly 200 million years. The most successful surviving group of gymnosperms are the conifers, which include such species as pines, spruces, firs, larches and junipers.

Most conifers are evergreen and have small needle-like or scale-like leaves which are adapted to withstand extreme temperature changes. Some species are deciduous, but most retain their leaves for two or more years before shedding them.

Reproduction

Most conifers produce cones – wood-like fruits that contain the male and female gametes. The male cones produce pollen that is carried by the wind to settle between the scales of female cones on other trees. The pollen stimulates ovules to change into seeds, and the scales of the female cone close up to protect the seeds. When the seeds are ripe, up to two years later, environmental conditions stimulate the cone to open its scales and the naked seeds to fall to the ground.

ANGIOSPERMS – THE FLOWERING PLANTS

Angiosperms first appeared in the fossil record around 130 million years ago. They quickly adapted to a wide variety of environments and succeeded gymnosperms as the dominant land plants. Their reproductive success was largely due to two key adaptations:

Advances Made Over Gymnosperms

1) They produced flowers which attracted pollinating agents such as insects and birds; and
2) They produced seeds encased in fruits to aid in seed dispersal.

Angiosperms are classified in two main groups:

1) Monocots – plants with one embryonic leaf at germination, parallel-veined leaves, stems with scattered vascular bundles with little or no cambium (group includes grasses, cattails, orchids and corn); and

2) Dicots – plants with two embryonic leaves at germination, net-veined leaves, stems with cylindrical vascular bundles in a regular pattern that contain cambium (group includes more than 200,000 species ranging from tiny herbs to huge trees).

Angiosperms make up a diverse and widespread group of plants ranging from trees and shrubs such as oaks, cherries, maples, hazelnuts and apples, to typical flowers like lilies, orchids, roses, daisies, and violets. The trees and shrubs within this group are commonly referred to as deciduous and most shed their leaves annually.

Reproduction

A typical flower has colorful petals that encircle the male and female reproductive structures (see illustration p. 109). The male stamens are composed of thin filaments supporting anthers containing pollen. The female pistil contains unfertilized seeds in the swollen basal part called the ovary. Pollination occurs when pollen, carried by the wind or animals, reaches the pistil.

Once fertilization has occurred, the ovules develop into seeds and the ovary into a fruit. The fruit and seeds mature together, with the fruit ripening to the point where the seeds are capable of germinating. At maturity, each seed contains an embryo and a food supply to nourish it upon germination. Upon ripening, the fruit may fall to the ground with the seeds still inside, as in peaches, cherries and squash, or it may burst open and scatter its seeds in the wind, like poplar trees, willows and dandelions.

Fruit comes in many forms, from grapes, tomatoes, apples and pears, to pea and bean pods, nuts, burrs and capsules. Regardless of its shape, fruit enhances the reproductive success of angiosperms in two important ways. First, it helps to protect the seeds from the elements until they have fully matured, enabling them to survive unfavorable conditions. Secondly, fruit aids in seed dispersal. Some fruits are eaten by animals that eventually release the seeds in their feces, an ideal growing medium. Others may be spiny or burred so they catch on the coats of animals, or may have special features which enable them to be carried away from their parent plant by the wind or water.

GEOLOGICAL TIMESCALE

ERA	PERIOD	MYA*	EVENTS
CENOZOIC	HOLOCENE	.01	Dominance of man.
CENOZOIC	QUATERNARY	2.5	First human civilizations.
CENOZOIC	TERTIARY	65	Mammals, birds, insects and angiosperms dominate the land.
MESOZOIC	CRETACEOUS	135	Dinosaurs extinct. Mammals, insects and angiosperms undergo great expansion. Gymnosperms decline.
MESOZOIC	JURASSIC	190	Age of Reptiles; dinosaurs dominant. First birds appear.
MESOZOIC	TRIASSIC	225	First dinosaurs and mammals appear. Gymnosperms are dominant plants.
PALEOZOIC	PERMIAN	280	Great expansion of reptiles causes amphibians to decline. Many marine invertebrates become extinct.
PALEOZOIC	CARBONIFEROUS	340	Age of Amphibians; amphibians dominant. First reptiles appear. Fishes undergo a great expansion.
PALEOZOIC	DEVONIAN	400	Age of Fishes; fishes dominant. First amphibians, insects and gymnosperms appear.
PALEOZOIC	SILURIAN	430	First jawed fishes appear. Plants move onto land.
PALEOZOIC	ORDOVICIAN	500	First vertebrates appear.
PALEOZOIC	CAMBRIAN	600	Marine invertebrates and algae abundant.

*Millions of years ago

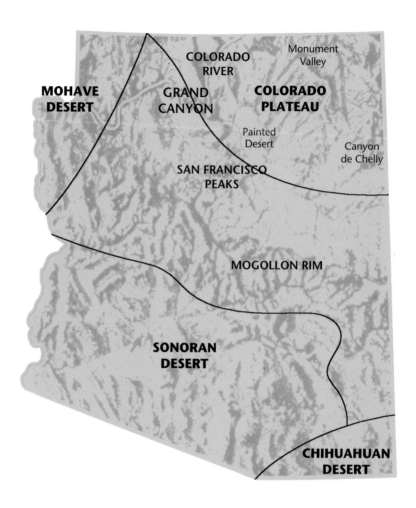

GEOGRAPHY

Highest Point: 12,670 ft. (3,851 m) Humphrey's Peak near Flagstaff
Lowest Point: 70 ft. (21 m) along the Colorado River
Area: 113,900 square miles (183,300 square km)

Outstanding Features

The Colorado Plateau and The Grand Canyon

Found in the northeastern quarter of the state, the Colorado Plateau is comprised of a series of more-or-less level plateaus separated by deep chasms. The area encompasses some of Arizona's most spectacular scenery including the Grand Canyon, Canyon de Chelly, Monument Valley and the Painted Desert.

The Mogollon Rim

The result of an upheaval in the earth's crust back in the Mesozoic Era, the Mogollon Rim (pronounced MUGGY-yone) is a vertical wall of rock up to 2,000 ft. (609 m) high that forms a natural barrier in east-central Arizona.

San Francisco Peaks

A trio of peaks north of Flagstaff are the remnants of what was once a huge volcano. Area has many notable geologic features including the 1,000 ft. (300 m) high Sunset Crater.

Deserts

Arizona is home to three distinct desert ecosystems – the Sonoran, Mohave, and Chihuahuan. Of these, the Sonoran is the largest, covering some 120,000 square miles (193,100 sq. km). Its rugged terrain, jagged peaks and stately saguaro cacti are symbolic of southwestern deserts.

The Colorado River

Over 700 miles of this mighty river flows through northeastern and western Arizona. Principal tributaries are the Gila, Little Colorado, Bill Williams, Verde, Salt and Santa Cruz rivers. Dams along the Colorado in western Arizona have created two of the country's longest lakes, Lake Mead and Lake Mohave. Ranging from the Rocky Mountains in Colorado to the Gulf of California, the Colorado and its lakes and reservoirs now supply over half of the western U.S. with fresh water.

GENERALIZED RELIEF

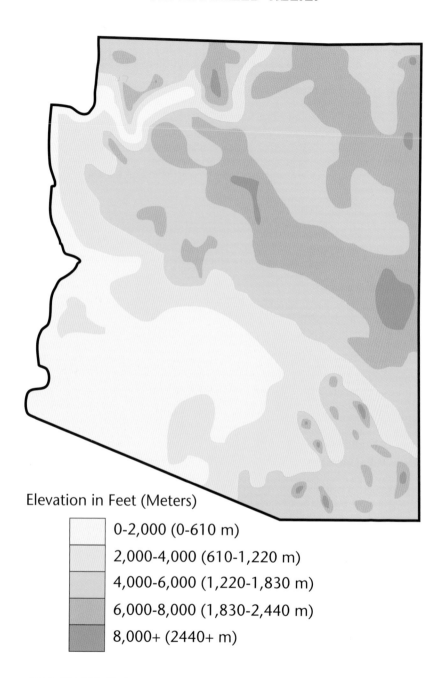

Elevation in Feet (Meters)

- 0-2,000 (0-610 m)
- 2,000-4,000 (610-1,220 m)
- 4,000-6,000 (1,220-1,830 m)
- 6,000-8,000 (1,830-2,440 m)
- 8,000+ (2440+ m)

LIFE ZONES

The following life zones are based on the Merriam system. The logic behind the system is that since plants require rainfall, and rainfall is greatly influenced by elevation, plants (and the species that rely on them) will tend to be found between certain elevations throughout the state. Elevations are not exact, and the zones are intended to provide a general idea of the habitats found in Arizona.

Lower Sonoran Zone – to 4,500 ft. (1,371 m)

Arizona's famous desert terrain encompasses barren mountains and dry plains. Cacti and drought-resistant plants like palo verde, ironwood and ocotillo are abundant. Many of the animals live underground in burrows where they rest during the heat of the day. Characteristic species include the coyote, kangaroo rat, jackrabbit, bighorn sheep, roadrunner, Gambel's quail, raven, cactus wren, woodpeckers, snakes and lizards.

Upper Sonoran Zone – 4,500-6500 ft. (1,371-1,981 m)

This zone receives enough rainfall to support grasslands and woodlands of stunted oaks and pinyon pines. In some parts of the state, chaparral vegetation like scrub oak and mountain mahogany grow in impenetrable thickets. Characteristic species include deer, javelina, pronghorn antelope and abundant reptiles.

Transition Zone – 6,500-8,000 ft. (1,371-2,438 m)

This zone is dominated by ponderosa pine forests. Species associated with forests including squirrels, rabbits, skunks, deer, elk, mountain lions, bears and forest birds like jays, juncos and turkeys.

Canadian Zone – 8,000-9,500 ft. (2,438-2,895 m)

Douglas-fir is the dominant plant in this zone and some attain heights of over 300 feet (91 m). Forests of spruce, fir and aspen are also found at this elevation. Resident species include deer, elk, bear, squirrels, jays and juncos.

Hudsonian Zone – 9,500-11,500 ft. (2,895-3,505 m)

With a growing season of less than four months, this zone is characterized by stunted (and often gnarled) trees and windswept slopes. Dominant trees are spruce, fir and bristlecone pine. The oldest known tree in the world is a bristlecone pine that is over 4,600 years old.

Alpine Zone – 11,500-12,670 ft. (3,505-3,862 m)

Also called arctic-alpine, this zone above the treeline is inhospitable to most plants and animals. Only about 75 species of cold-resistant herbs, grasses and lichens are able to grow here and animals are virtually nonexistent.

PRECIPITATION

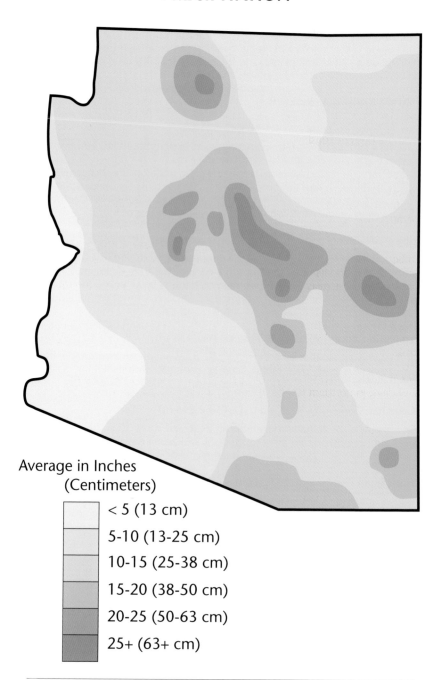

Average in Inches
(Centimeters)

- < 5 (13 cm)
- 5-10 (13-25 cm)
- 10-15 (25-38 cm)
- 15-20 (38-50 cm)
- 20-25 (50-63 cm)
- 25+ (63+ cm)

CLIMATE

Average Annual Rainfall:	13 inches (30 cm)
Average July Temperature:	Phoenix 92° F (33° C)
	Flagstaff 66° F (19° C)
Average January Temperature:	Phoenix 52° F (11° C)
	Flagstaff 28° F (-2° C)
Average Days of Sunshine:	Phoenix > 300

Arizona's climate varies with its geography, although sunny, dry weather prevails throughout the state. As a rule, the temperature drops 3.5° F (1.95 C°) for every thousand feet in elevation gained. In desert regions, the temperature can vary over 40° F (22° C) in a single day.

Arizona has two rainy seasons in winter and late summer. Winter rains tend to be steady, in contrast to the explosive summer thunderstorms. The vast majority of thunderstorms are localized and less than three miles in diameter. They often cause heavy runoff and flash flooding of stream beds and roadways.

The mountains and high plateaus are considerably cooler than the desert regions and receive up to five times the rainfall. In winter, some mountain areas receive up to 8 ft. (2.4 m) of snowfall annually.

The mild climate in southern Arizona provides for a growing season of 240 days. In northern reaches it may be as short as 100 days.

WHAT ARE MAMMALS?

Most mammals are warm-blooded, furred creatures that have 4 limbs and a tail, 5 digits on each foot, and several different kinds of teeth. All North American species give birth to live young which feed on milk from their mother's mammary glands.

HOW TO IDENTIFY MAMMALS

Mammals are generally secretive in their habits and therefore difficult to spot in the field. The best time to look for mammals is at dusk, dawn and at night, since many retreat to burrows during the day to escape the heat. Some of the best places to look for them are in undisturbed areas affording some source of cover such as wood edges and scrub thickets.

When you spot a mammal, consider its size, shape and color. Check for distinguishing field marks and note the surrounding habitat.

COMMON TRACKS

Studying tracks is an easy way to discover the kinds of mammals found in your area. For more information on animal tracks, see the references under mammals in the back of the guide.

Jackrabbit

Mouse

Squirrel

Prairie Dog

Bobcat

Raccoon

Skunk

Coyote

Kangaroo Rat

Mule Deer

Bighorn Sheep

Black Bear

Javelina

N.B. – *Tracks are not to scale*

INSECTIVORES

Insectivores are generally small mammals with long snouts, short legs and sharp teeth. They live on or under the ground and feed on insects and other invertebrates.

DESERT SHREW
Notiosorex crawfordi
Size: 3-4 in. (8-10 cm)
Description: Grayish, mouse-like mammal with a long, pointed nose.
Habitat: Desert scrub.
Comments: Obtains water from the insects it feeds on. Like all shrews, it has a very high metabolic rate and may eat up to twice its weight in food each day.

BATS

The only true flying mammals, bats have large ears, small eyes and broad wings. Primarily nocturnal, they have developed a sophisticated sonar system – echolocation – to help them hunt insects at night. As they fly, they emit a series of high-frequency sounds that bounce off objects and tell them what lies in their path. During daylight, they seek refuge in caves, trees and attics. Rarely harmful, bats are valuable in helping check insect populations.

BRAZILIAN FREE-TAILED BAT
Tadarida brasiliensis
Size: 2-4 in. (5-10 cm)
Description: Small chocolate-brown bat with velvety fur and a tail extending beyond the wing membrane.
Habitat: Roosts in caves and buildings.
Comments: Typically lives in large colonies of several thousand individuals.

WESTERN PIPISTRELLE
Pipistrellus hesperus
Size: 1.5-3.5 in. (4-9 cm)
Description: Pale coat is grayish to red-brown above and whitish below.
Habitat: Caves, buildings, deserts, rocky areas.
Comments: The smallest U.S. bat. Typically appears early in the evening, often before sundown. Flight is erratic.

HOARY BAT
Lasiurus cinereus
Size: 4-6 in. (10-15 cm)
Description: Dark brown fur is heavily frosted with white. Tail membrane is furred.
Habitat: Wooded areas.
Comments: Note large size. Roosts in tree foliage during the day. A migratory bat, it winters in South America.

RABBITS & ALLIES

Members of this distinctive group of mammals have long ears, large eyes and long hind legs. They commonly rest in protected areas like thickets during the day. When threatened, they thump their hind feet on the ground as an alarm signal.

DESERT COTTONTAIL
Sylvilagus audubonii
Size: 14-17 in. (35-43 cm)
Description: Coat is buff-brown above, white below. Note rusty nape and white tail. Ears are large.
Habitat: Open areas in deserts and grasslands, residential areas.
Comments: Active day and night, it feeds on a range of plants including grasses, mesquite and cacti. Uses stumps and sloping trees as lookouts.

EASTERN COTTONTAIL
Sylvilagus floridanus
Size: 14-18 in. (35-45 cm)
Description: Gray-brown bunny has a white, cottony tail. Nape of neck is rusty.
Habitat: Thick brushy areas, fields.
Comments: Feeds primarily on grass. Most active at dawn and dusk, it rests in thickets during the day. Females have up to 7 litters a year of 1-9 young.

BLACK-TAILED JACKRABBIT
Lepus californicus
Size: 18-25 in. (45-63 cm)
Description: Large gray or tan rabbit with long black-tipped ears and a black-streaked tail.
Habitat: Open areas in deserts and grasslands.
Comments: Very athletic, it hops up to 10 ft. (3 m) at a time and reaches speeds up to 35 mph (56 kph). The similar antelope jackrabbit (*L. alleni*), found in south-central Arizona, lacks black-tipped ears.

SQUIRRELS & ALLIES

This diverse family of hairy-tailed, large-eyed rodents includes chipmunks, tree squirrels, ground squirrels and marmots. Most are active during the day and are easily observed in the field. Note that size includes tail length.

CLIFF CHIPMUNK
Tamias dorsalis
Size: 8-11 in. (20-28 cm)
Description: Grayish, with indistinct stripes on back, sides and face (may be absent in some). Feet are yellowish.
Habitat: Pinyon pine/juniper zones, rocky areas.
Comments: Active during the day, it is very vocal and often heard twittering and chattering. Feeds on seeds, berries and nuts.

ABERT'S SQUIRREL
Sciurus aberti
Size: 17-23 in. (43-58 cm)
Description: Large, tassel-eared gray squirrel with a white belly.
Habitat: Coniferous forests.
Comments: Feeds primarily on conifer seeds and nuts. A related subspecies, the Kaibab squirrel (*S.a. kaibabensis*), has a white tail and is found only on the North Rim of the Grand Canyon.

ROCK SQUIRREL
Spermophilus variegatus
Size: 17-21 in. (43-53 cm)
Description: Large mottled grayish ground squirrel with a long, bushy tail.
Habitat: Rocky canyons and slopes.
Comments: Often seen sitting on rocks, watching for danger. Unlike many ground-dwelling squirrels, it climbs trees easily.

HARRIS' ANTELOPE SQUIRREL
Ammospermophilus harrisii
Size: 8-10 in. (20-25 cm)
Description: The only chipmunk-like mammal found in the desert region. White side stripe is key field mark.
Habitat: Low deserts and foothills.
Comments: Holds tail aloft while running, using it as an umbrella to cut the sun. Active throughout the day.

ROUND-TAILED GROUND SQUIRREL
Spermophilus tereticaudus
Size: 8-11 in. (20-28 cm)
Description: Cinnamon to grayish squirrel with slender, round tail.
Habitat: Low desert region in southern Arizona.
Comments: Active morning and evening. Very common in some areas.

ARIZONA GRAY SQUIRREL
Sciurus arizonensis
Size: 20-22 in. (50-55 cm)
Description: Gray squirrel has a white belly. Long tail has a white fringe.
Habitat: High country forests in western and southern Arizona.
Comments: Feeds on acorns, nuts, juniper berries and seeds.

RED SQUIRREL
Tamiasciurus hudsonicus
Size: 11-15 in. (28-38 cm)
Description: Rusty-olive squirrel has a whitish belly and under-parts. Bushy tail is orangish.
Habitat: Forests in northern and western Arizona.
Comments: Active during the day, it is very vocal and often heard twittering and chattering. Feeds on seeds, berries and nuts. Spends much of the summer caching winter food stores.

GUNNISON'S PRAIRIE DOG
Cynomys gunnisoni
Size: 12-15 in. (30-38 cm)
Description: A cat-sized, chunky squirrel with a short, white-tipped tail. Presence is detected by bare mounds of earth with numerous burrow openings.
Habitat: Open grasslands in northern Arizona.
Comments: One of the most gregarious mammals, it lives in colonies of up to several hundred individuals. The similar black-tailed prairie dog (*C. ludovicianus*) is rarely spotted in southeastern Arizona.

POCKET GOPHERS

These mole-like mammals are well known for the mounds of dirt they push up when excavating their burrows. They are named for their fur-lined, external cheek pouches that they stuff with food or nesting material.

BOTTA'S POCKET GOPHER
Thomomys bottae
Size: 6-11 in. (15-28 cm)
Description: Distinguished by prominent, crescent-shaped claws and brown-gray coat.
Habitat: Found throughout Arizona in areas with soft soil.
Comments: Feeds underground by cutting off the stems of plants below the surface and pulling them into the burrow.

MICE & ALLIES

Most members of this large group have large ears, long tails and breed throughout the year. Dedicated omnivores, they have adapted to practically every North American habitat. Sizes noted include tail length.

DEER MOUSE
Peromyscus maniculatus
Size: 4-8 in. (10-20 cm)
Description: Bicolored coat is pale gray to red-brown above and white below. Tail is hairy and bicolored.
Habitat: Common and widespread in a variety of habitats.
Comments: Feeds on a variety of foods including seeds, buds, fruit and invertebrates. Active year-round.

CACTUS MOUSE
Peromyscus eremicus
Size: 6-8 in. (15-20 cm)
Description: Large-eared, long-tailed mouse is gray above, whitish below. Tail is sparsely haired.
Habitat: Throughout the desert region.
Comments: Feeds primarily on seeds and insects. Nocturnal and very common in certain areas.

HOUSE MOUSE
Mus musculus
Size: 5-8 in. (13-20 cm)
Description: Told by its brown to grayish coat, large eyes and ears and scaly tail.
Habitat: Near human dwellings.
Comments: Normally lives in colonies. Females have up to 5 litters of 4-8 young annually.

ORD'S KANGAROO RAT
Dipodomys ordii
Size: 8-11 in. (20-28 cm)
Description: Distinguished by its large hind feet and long tail. Coat is buff above, white below.
Habitat: Open areas with sandy soils.
Comments: Capable of leaping 6-8 ft. (1.8-2.4 m) in a single bound. Active year-round, it feeds on the seeds of mesquite, sunflowers and other plants. Three similar species of kangaroo rat are found in Arizona.

NORWAY RAT
Rattus norvegicus
Size: 12-18 in. (30-45 cm)
Description: Large gray-brown rodent with a scaly tail.
Habitat: Common near human dwellings.
Comments: Albino strains of this species are commonly used in lab experiments. The all-black black rat (*Rattus rattus*) – also known as a roof rat – is also found in Arizona.

Norway Rat

Black Rat

MUSKRAT
Ondatra zibethicus
Size: 16-24 in. (40-60 cm)
Description: Often mistaken for beavers, these aquatic rodents are smaller and have a long, scaly tail that is flattened on either side.
Habitat: Marshes, lakes, waterways.
Comments: In swampy areas, they construct dome-shaped houses of marsh vegetation up to 3 ft. (90 cm) high. Feeds primarily on aquatic plants. Active year-round.

WHITE-THROATED WOODRAT
Neotoma albigula
Size: 12-16 in. (30-40 cm)
Description: Large gray-brown rat with light underparts, a white throat and white feet.
Habitat: Brushy areas of foothills and deserts.
Comments: Often builds large houses of sticks or cactus parts beneath plants or in rock crevices. Obtains all its water from the cacti and leafy plants it feeds on.

PORCUPINES

Porcupines are medium-sized mammals with coats of stiff, barbed quills. When threatened, they face away from their aggressor, erect the quills and lash out with their tail. The loosely rooted quills detach on contact and are extremely difficult to remove.

COMMON PORCUPINE
Erethizon dorsatum
Size: 25-37 in. (63-93 cm)
Description: Told by its chunky profile, arched back and long gray coat of barbed quills.
Habitat: Forests, shrubby ravines and sometimes deserts.
Comments: Spends much of its time in trees feeding on leaves, twigs and bark.

RACCOONS & ALLIES

All members of this diverse family of mammals have ringed tails.

COMMON RACCOON
Procyon lotor
Size: 25-37 in. (63-93 cm)
Description: Gray-brown coat, black mask and ringed tail.
Habitat: Wooded areas near water.
Comments: Feeds on small animals, insects, plants and refuse. Often dunks its food into water before eating it. Primarily nocturnal.

RINGTAIL
Bassariscus astutus
Size: 24-32 in. (60-80 cm)
Description: Has large eyes, large ears and a long, ringed tail. Lacks a black mask.
Habitat: Rocky areas, rough country, chaparral.
Comments: Hunts at night, killing prey with a bite to the neck. Nicknamed 'Miners' Cats,' they were once used like cats to control rodent populations in mines.

Arizona's State Mammal

COATI
Nasua narica
Size: 33-52 in. (83-130 cm)
Description: Long-tailed, gray-brown animal with a long, pointed snout. Tail is nearly same length as body.
Habitat: Woodlands of lower mountain canyons in southeastern and south-central Arizona.
Comments: Walks with tail held aloft. Active during the day, it travels in large groups of a dozen or more individuals.

SKUNKS & ALLIES

Members of this group usually have small heads, long necks, short legs and long bodies. All but sea otters have prominent anal scent glands which are used for social and sexual communication.

STRIPED SKUNK
Mephitis mephitis
Size: 20-31 in. (50-78 cm)
Description: Black mammal with thin white forehead stripe and two white back stripes.
Habitat: Wooded areas near water.
Comments: Protects itself by spraying aggressors with noxious-smelling musk from its anal glands. Spray effective to 20 ft. (6 m). Feeds on vegetation, insects and small mammals.

WESTERN SPOTTED SKUNK
Spilogale putorius
Size: 9-19 in. (23-48 cm)
Description: Black coat has 4-6 irregular stripes. White spots on head and sides.
Habitat: Rocky areas, woodlands.
Comments: When threatened, it gives warning by raising its tail, doing a handstand and spreading its hind feet before spraying. A good climber and swimmer, it is more agile than larger skunks.

AMERICAN BADGER
Taxidea taxus
Size: 20-34 in. (50-85 cm)
Description: A squat, heavy-bodied animal with a long yellow-gray to brown coat, white forehead stripe and long foreclaws.
Habitat: Grasslands and uncultivated pastures, deserts.
Comments: A prodigious burrower that feeds mostly on ground squirrels and other burrowing mammals.

BEAVER

Found on rivers, lakes and marshes, beavers are the largest North American rodents. Highly aquatic, they have webbed feet and long, broad tails which they slap on the water's surface when alarmed.

AMERICAN BEAVER
Castor canadensis
Size: 40-48 in. (1-1.2 m)
Description: Glossy brown coat, flat, scaly tail.
Habitat: Lakes, ponds and streams.
Comments: Many beavers live in dens excavated along banks; others build cone-shaped houses (lodges) of sticks and mud. Diet consists of the bark of deciduous trees and shrubs, including aspens, willows and maples.

DOG-LIKE MAMMALS

Members of this family have long snouts, erect ears and resemble domestic dogs in looks and habit. All are active year-round.

COMMON GRAY FOX
Urocyon cinereoargenteus
Size: 30-44 in. (75-110 cm)
Description: Distinguished by its coat that is blackish-gray above and rusty-white below. Tail has black tip.
Habitat: Deserts, oak woodlands, forests.
Comments: A secretive, nocturnal species, it sometimes forages during the day. An excellent climber, it often seeks refuge in trees.

KIT FOX
Vulpes velox
Size: 24-31 in. (60-78 cm)
Description: Small, large-eared fox with a buff-colored coat.
Habitat: Grasslands and deserts.
Comments: Primarily nocturnal, it can be spotted on roadsides at night in low desert areas. Eats rodents, birds and insects. Once common, it is now in danger of extinction.

COYOTE
Canis latrans
Size: 40-52 in. (1-1.3 m)
Description: Yellow-gray dog with a pointed nose, rust-colored legs and ears and a bushy, black-tipped tail.
Habitat: Variable, from deserts to forests.
Comments: It runs with its tail held down and can often be seen loping across fields and along roadsides at dawn and dusk.

CAT-LIKE MAMMALS

These highly specialized carnivores are renowned hunters. All have short faces, keen vision, powerful bodies and retractable claws. Most are nocturnal hunters.

BOBCAT
Lynx rufus
Size: 3-4 ft. (.9-1.2 m)
Description: Told by its spotted red-brown coat and short, black-striped tail.
Habitat: Wide range of habitats from deserts to canyons in foothills.
Comments: Named for its bobbed tail, it rests in thickets by day and hunts rabbits and rodents by night.

MOUNTAIN LION
Felis concolor
Size: 5-9 ft. (1.5-2.7 m)
Description: Large tan cat has a whitish belly and long, black-tipped tail.
Habitat: Primarily mountainous areas.
Comments: A solitary hunter, it feeds on hoofed mammals, hares and other small mammals. Also called cougar and puma.

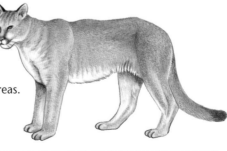

BEARS

This group includes the largest terrestrial carnivores in the world. All are heavy-bodied, large-headed animals, with short ears and small tails. Their sense of smell is keen, although their eyesight is generally poor.

BLACK BEAR
Ursus americanus
Size: 4-6 ft. (1.2-1.8 m)
Description: Coat is normally black, but cinnamon and blue-gray variants also occur.
Habitat: Primarily mountainous areas.
Comments: Diet is 85% vegetarian and consists of berries, vegetation, fish, insects, mammals and refuse. Its tracks can sometimes be spotted in muddy areas near water. Found in mountainous areas of central and southern Arizona.

HOOFED MAMMALS

This general grouping includes odd- and even-toed hoofed mammals from a variety of families.

MULE DEER
Odocoileus hemionus
Size: 4-8 ft. (1.2-2.4 m)
Description: Distinguished by its large 'mule-sized' ears and black-tipped tail.
Habitat: Lives in mountainous regions in summer, and grasslands and deserts in winter.
Comments: Feeds mostly on shrubs, twigs and grasses. Males shed antlers January-March.

WHITE-TAILED DEER
Odocoileus virginianus
Size: 6-7 ft. (1.8-2.1 m)
Description: Coat is tan in summer, grayish in winter. Named for its large, white-edged tail which is held aloft, flag-like, when running.
Habitat: Forests, farmlands and river valleys.
Comments: An agile, elusive deer, it can reach speeds of 40 mph (65 kph) and leap obstacles as high as 8 ft. (2.5 m). Most active at dawn and dusk.

DESERT BIGHORN SHEEP
Ovis canadensis mexicana
Size: 5-6 ft. (1.5-1.8 m)
Description: Told by its coiled horns and white rump patch.
Habitat: Rocky, rugged areas near water.
Comments: Desert subspecies is uniquely adapted to its environment and can live for up to a week between waterings.

PRONGHORN
Antilocapra americana
Size: 4-5 ft. (1.2-1.5 m)
Description: A tan, deer-like animal with white throat bands, a white rump, and stumpy, pronged horns.
Habitat: Grasslands and sagebrush flats.
Comments: The fastest animal in North America, it has been clocked at speeds up to 70 mph (112 kph).

JAVELINA
Tayassu tajacu
Size: 34-40 in. (85-100 cm)
Description: Pig-like animal with a dark, bristly coat.
Habitat: Well-vegetated deserts in southern Arizona.
Comments: Feeds on cacti, seeds, fruit, small animals (including snakes, birds and rodents) and invertebrates. Primarily nocturnal.

ELK
Cervus canadensis
Size: 6-9 ft. (1.8-2.7 m)
Description: Distinguished by large size, shaggy brown neck and light rump patch.
Habitat: Mountain meadows and open forests.
Comments: Fairly common in central highlands of Arizona.

WHAT ARE BIRDS?

Birds are warm-blooded, feathered animals with two wings and two legs. The majority can fly and those that cannot are believed to be descended from ancestors that did. Adaptations for flight include hollow bones and an enhanced breathing capacity. Birds also have an efficient 4-chambered heart and are insulated against the weather to enhance temperature regulation.

HOW TO IDENTIFY BIRDS

As with other species, the best way to become good at identifying birds is simply to practice. The more birds you attempt to identify, the better you will become at distinguishing species.

When birding, the first thing to note is the habitat you are exploring, in order to know what kinds of birds to expect. When you spot a bird, check for obvious field marks. Note the shape of its silhouette and beak. Note the color and pattern of its feathers for distinguishing markings at rest and in flight. Is it small (sparrow), medium (crow), or large (heron)? Does it have any unusual behavioral characteristics?

If you are interested in enhancing your field skills, it is essential to become familiar with bird songs since many species that are difficult to observe in the field are readily identified by their distinctive song. Bird song tapes and CDs are available from nature stores and libraries.

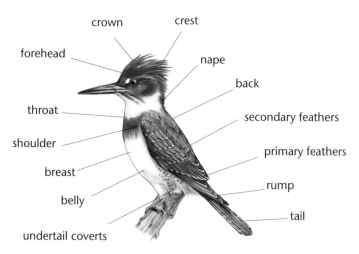

N.B. – *It is important to note that many species illustrations feature the adult male in its breeding coloration. Colors and markings shown may be duller or absent during different times of the year.*

GREBES

The members of this group of duck-like birds have short tails, slender necks and stiff bills. Excellent divers, they have lobed toes rather than webbed feet.

PIED-BILLED GREBE
Podilymbus podiceps
Size: 12-15 in. (30-38 cm)
Description: Distinguished by its small size and black-banded, chicken-like white bill.
Habitat: Ponds, marshes and lakes.
Comments: Often swims with body partially submerged. Hatchlings are often carried and fed on the backs of their parents.

PELICANS & ALLIES

These web-footed birds are common on large lakes.

DOUBLE-CRESTED CORMORANT
Phalacrocorax auritus
Size: 30-36 in. (75-90 cm)
Description: Glossy black bird with a slender neck, hooked bill and red throat pouch.
Habitat: Large lakes and rivers.
Comments: Nests in colonies and is often seen perched on trees and pilings near marinas. Often perches with wings out-stretched to allow them to dry.

AMERICAN WHITE PELICAN
Pelecanus erythrorhynchos
Size: To 6 ft. (1.8 m)
Description: Large, stout white bird has a long bill and an orange-yellow throat pouch. Wing tips are black.
Habitat: Large lakes.
Comments: Often travels in flocks that fly in a V-formation. Feeds by scooping small schooling fish into its throat pouch.

HERONS & ALLIES

Large wading birds with long legs, long necks and slender bills. Sexes are similar. All fly with their necks folded into an 'S' curve.

GREAT BLUE HERON
Ardea herodias
Size: 40-52 in. (1-1.3 m)
Description: Large, slender grayish-blue bird with long legs, a long, yellowish bill and white face. Black plumes extend back from the eye.
Habitat: Wetlands, margins of ponds, lakes and watercourses.
Comments: Often seen stalking fish and frogs in shallow water.

Green Heron

GREEN HERON
Butorides virescens
Size: To 22 in. (55 cm)
Description: Gray-green wading bird has a chestnut neck, a black crown and yellow legs.
Habitat: Ponds, streams, brackish marshes.
Comments: One of a number of herons found stalking fish and frogs in the shallows. Another Arizona heron is the black-and-white black-crowned night-heron (*Nycticorax nycticorax*).

Black-crowned Night-Heron

Great Egret

Snowy Egret

GREAT EGRET
Ardea alba
Size: To 40 in. (1 m)
Description: Large white bird with a yellow bill, black legs and black feet.
Habitat: Variable throughout Arizona.
Comments: Usually feeds by stalking prey in shallow water. The similar snowy egret (*Egretta thula*) is about 12 in. (30 cm) shorter and has a black bill and yellow feet. The stockier, yellow-billed cattle egret (*Bubulcus ibis*: 20 in./50 cm) is the common egret seen feeding on lawns and fields.

GEESE

Geese are large, long-necked birds found near ponds and marshes. Highly terrestrial, they are often spotted grazing in fields and meadows. Their diet consists largely of grasses, grains and some aquatic plants. Noisy in flight, they are often heard before they are seen passing overhead.

CANADA GOOSE
Branta canadensis
Size: 24-45 in. (60-114 cm)
Description: Told by black head and neck, and white cheek patch.
Habitat: Near marshes, ponds, lakes and rivers.
Comments: Geese fly in a V-formation when migrating. Pairs usually mate for life. Call is a nasal – *honk*.

DUCKS & ALLIES

Smaller than geese, ducks have shorter necks and are primarily aquatic. In most, breeding males are more brightly colored than females. Both sexes have a brightly-colored band (speculum) on the trailing edge of the wing.

NORTHERN SHOVELER
Anas clypeata
Size: 17-20 in. (43-50 cm)
Description: Told by its flat head and large, spatulate bill. Male has a green head, rusty sides and a blue wing patch.
Habitat: Fresh- and saltwater marshes, lakes, ponds.
Comments: Shovel-shaped bill is used to strain aquatic animals and vegetation from the water. Swims with bill pointed downward.

CINNAMON TEAL
Anas cyanoptera
Size: 14-17 in. (35-43 cm)
Description: Both sexes have a chalky blue forewing patch. Males are bright cinnamon; females are mottled brown.
Habitat: Marshes, shallow ponds and rivers.
Comments: The forewing patches are most visible in flight.

MALLARD
Anas platyrhynchos
Size: 20-28 in. (50-70 cm)
Description: Male has green head, white collar and chestnut breast. Female is mottled brown. Both have a metallic blue speculum.
Habitat: Ponds and marshes.
Comments: The ancestor of domestic ducks. Call is a loud – *quack*.

NORTHERN PINTAIL
Anas acuta
Size: 20-30 in. (50-75 cm)
Description: Distinguished by its long neck and pointed tail. Male has a white breast and a white neck stripe. Both sexes have a glossy brown speculum which is bordered in white.
Habitat: Shallow marshes and ponds.
Comments: Call is a short whistle.

GREEN-WINGED TEAL
Anas crecca
Size: 12-16 in. (30-40 cm)
Description: Male has chestnut head and a green eye patch. Female is brown-gray with a green speculum.
Habitat: Lakes and ponds.
Comments: Fast fliers that travel in tight flocks.

COOTS

Coots are chicken-billed birds often found in the company of ducks and geese. They are, however, more closely related to cranes than ducks.

AMERICAN COOT
Fulica americana
Size: 13-16 in. (33-40 cm)
Description: Dark bird with a chicken-like white bill, white rump, long greenish legs and lobed toes.
Habitat: Lakes, ponds and marshes.
Comments: Feeds on the shore and in the water. Habitually pumps its head back and forth when swimming.

HAWKS, EAGLES & ALLIES

Primarily carnivorous, these birds have sharp talons for grasping prey and sharply hooked bills for tearing into flesh. Many soar on wind currents when hunting. Sexes are similar in most.

Turkey Vulture

TURKEY VULTURE
Cathartes aura
Size: 26-32 in. (65-80 cm)
Description: Large, brown-black bird with a naked red head. Trailing half of wings are silvery.
Habitat: Dry, open country.
Comments: A common sight in southwest skies, it glides with its wings held in a slight V. The rare and endangered vulture, the California condor (*Gymnogyps californianus*) is being reintroduced to the wild in the Grand Canyon.

Condor

GOLDEN EAGLE
Aquila chrysaetos
Size: 30-41 in. (75-104 cm)
Description: Large, dark soaring bird with long, broad wings. Size distinguishes it from smaller hawks.
Habitat: Mountain regions.
Comments: Feeds on mammals, some birds and carrion. Often builds nests on power poles.

RED-TAILED HAWK
Buteo jamaicensis
Size: 20-25 in. (50-63 cm)
Description: Dark, broad-winged, wide-tailed hawk with light underparts and a red tail.
Habitat: Open fields and forests, farmlands.
Comments: This familiar hawk is often spotted perched on roadside poles and fence posts.

Black

Harris's

COMMON BLACK-HAWK
Buteogallus anthracinus
Size: 20-23 in. (50-58 cm)
Description: Black hawk has a prominent white tail band.
Habitat: Open woodlands, along waterways, canyons.
Comments: Often perches for long periods in trees when seeking prey. Call is a loud whistle. The band-tailed Harris's hawk (*Parabuteo unicinctus*) is common in southern Arizona.

OSPREY
Pandion haliaetus
Size: 20-25 in. (50-63 cm)
Description: Large hawk with dark brown back, light underparts and a dark eye stripe.
Habitat: Coastal, inland lakes and rivers.
Comments: Unlike most soaring birds, it glides with its wings arched. Often hovers over the water before diving after fish.

BALD EAGLE
Haliaeetus leucocephalus
Size: 30-43 in. (75-109 cm)
Description: Large dark bird with a white head and tail, and yellow legs and bill.
Habitat: Near water.
Comments: Feeds on fish and water birds. An endangered species, its local populations are well on the road to recovery.

AMERICAN KESTREL
Falco sparverius
Size: 9-12 in. (23-30 cm)
Description: Small falcon with a rusty back and tail, and pointed, narrow, spotted blue wings. Males have black facial marks.
Habitat: A variety of open habitats in urban and rural settings.
Comments: Formerly called the sparrow hawk. Often pumps its tail when perching.

CHICKEN-LIKE BIRDS

Ground-dwelling birds that are chicken-like in looks and habit. Most have stout bills, rounded wings and heavy bodies. Primarily ground-dwelling, they are capable of short bursts of flight.

WILD TURKEY
Meleagris gallopavo
Size: 34-48 in. (85-120 cm)
Description: Large dark bird with a bluish head, red wattles and a rusty tail.
Habitat: Oak and pine woodlands.
Comments: Call is similar to a barnyard turkey. Feeds on acorns, fruit and seeds and roosts in trees at night. Is Arizona's largest game bird.

GAMBEL'S QUAIL
Callipepla gambelii
Size: 9-12 in. (23-30 cm)
Description: Plump bird with blue chest, buff belly and forward-curving plume (teardrop topknot). Male has black face and belly patches.
Habitat: Deserts.
Comments: One of the more commonly observed desert birds, it typically scurries around the desert floor in coveys (small groups). The grayish, crested scaled quail (*Callipepla squamata*) is common in SE Arizona.

Gambel's

Scaled

PLOVERS

Related to shorebirds, these birds are distinguished by their thick necks, short bills and large eyes. They characteristically move about in quick short sprints. Sexes are similar.

KILLDEER
Charadrius vociferus
Size: 9-11 in. (23-28 cm)
Description: Brown bird with white breast and two black neck bands.
Habitat: Open areas near water in urban and rural settings.
Comments: Shrill call – *kill-dee, kill-dee* – is repeated continuously. Adults will often feign injury to lead intruders away from their nesting area.

DOVES

These familiar birds are common and widespread. All species coo. They feed largely on seeds, grain and insects.

ROCK PIGEON
Columba livia
Size: 12-13 in. (30-33 cm)
Description: Blue-gray bird with a white rump and black-banded tail. White, tan and brown variants also exist.
Habitat: Common in urban and rural settings.
Comments: One of the few birds that comes in a variety of colors and patterns, a result of selective breeding of captive birds.

MOURNING DOVE
Zenaida macroura
Size: 11-13 in. (28-33 cm)
Description: Slender tawny bird with a long, pointed tail.
Habitat: Open woodlands, urban areas.
Comments: Named for its mournful, cooing song. Often seen perched on powerlines beside roads. The most widespread and abundant dove in the U.S.

WHITE-WINGED DOVE
Zenaida asiatica
Size: 10-13 in. (25-33 cm)
Description: Drab brown dove told at a glance by its prominent white wing patches.
Habitat: Deserts, open woodlands.
Comments: Often seen perched on cacti in southern Arizona. Fast fliers, they are popular game birds.

INCA DOVE
Columbina inca
Size: 7-8 in. (18-20 cm)
Description: Small dove with fluffy plumage, chestnut wing patches and a long, white-edged tail.

Habitat: Primarily urban areas.
Comments: Commonly seen in residential areas, they form large flocks during the fall and winter.

ROADRUNNER & ALLIES

Members have long tails and curved bills. Sexes are similar.

GREATER ROADRUNNER
Geococcyx californianus
Size: 20-24 in. (50-60 cm)
Description: Long-legged, gray-brown bird with a crested head and long tail.
Habitat: Open areas in habitats including deserts and oak woodlands.
Comments: A ground-dwelling bird, it can maintain speeds of 15 mph (24 kph) while running. Feeds on small mammals, snakes and insects. Often spotted darting across desert roads after prey.

OWLS

These square-shaped birds of prey have large heads, large eyes and hooked bills. Sexes are similar.

GREAT HORNED OWL
Bubo virginianus
Size: 20-25 in. (50-63 cm)
Description: Large, dark brown bird with heavily barred plumage, ear tufts, yellow eyes and a white throat.
Habitat: Forests, deserts and urban areas.
Comments: Primarily nocturnal, it feeds on small mammals and birds. Sometimes spotted hunting during the day. Call is a deep, resonant – *hoo-hoo-hooooo*.

ELF OWL
Micrathene whitneyi
Size: 5-6 in. (13-15 cm)
Description: Tiny owl with white eyebrows, yellow eyes and a short tail.
Habitat: Saguaro desert, wooded canyons in southern Arizona.
Comments: Primarily nocturnal, it roosts by day in abandoned woodpecker holes in saguaro cacti or trees.

GOATSUCKERS

These nocturnal insect-eaters have large, swallow-like heads. Ancients believed that the birds used their huge gaping mouths to suck the milk of goats.

LESSER NIGHTHAWK
Chordeiles minor
Size: 8-9 in. (20-23 cm)
Description: Dull brown bird has a white throat. White wing tips are visible in flight.
Habitat: Forests, open country, cities.
Comments: Spectacular fliers, they can often be seen hawking for insects around streetlights at dusk.

HUMMINGBIRDS

The smallest birds, hummingbirds are named for the noise made by their wings during flight. All have long, needle-like bills and long tongues which are used to extract nectar from flowers.

BLACK-CHINNED HUMMINGBIRD
Archilochus alexandri
Size: 3-4 in. (8-10 cm)
Description: Small metallic green bird with a black chin and a purplish neck band. Females lack chin and neck markings.
Habitat: Urban areas, wooded canyons to middle elevations.
Comments: Southeastern Arizona attracts more species of hummingbird than anywhere else in the U.S. This is the most common summer species in southern Arizona.

ANNA'S HUMMINGBIRD
Calypte anna
Size: 3-4 in. (8-10 cm)
Description: Small, metallic-green bird. Male has red throat and head. Female has spotted throat.
Habitat: Urban areas, wooded canyons to middle elevations.
Comments: Subsists on a diet of nectar, insects and spiders. Many desert plants rely on hummingbirds for pollination.

KINGFISHERS

Solitary, broad-billed birds renowned for their fishing expertise.

BELTED KINGFISHER
Megaceryle alcyon
Size: 10-14 in. (25-35 cm)
Description: Stocky, crested blue-gray bird with a large head and bill.
Habitat: Near wooded ponds, lakes and rivers.
Comments: Often seen perched over clear water. Hovers over water before plunging in headfirst after fish.

WOODPECKERS

These strong-billed birds are usually spotted on tree trunks chipping away bark in search of insects. All have stiff tails that act like props as they forage. In spring, males drum on dead limbs and other resonant objects (e.g. garbage cans, drainpipes) to establish their territories.

NORTHERN FLICKER
Colaptes auratus
Size: 10-13 in. (25-33 cm)
Description: Brownish woodpecker with a spotted breast and black bib. 'Yellow-shafted' morphs have a red nape patch and yellow wing linings; males have a black 'mustache'. 'Red-shafted' morphs have reddish wing linings; males have a red 'mustache'.
Habitat: Rural and urban woodlands, desert.
Comments: The similar gilded flicker (*C. chrysoides*), common in the desert southwest, has yellow wing and tail linings.

Red-shafted   Gilded

GILA WOODPECKER
Melanerpes uropygialis
Size: 8-10 in. (20-25 cm)
Description: Medium-sized woodpecker with a tan head and belly and a black-and-white-checked back. Male has a red cap.
Habitat: Urban areas, along desert creeks.
Comments: Common in the Sonoran Desert, it nests in holes in saguaro cacti.

ACORN WOODPECKER
Melanerpes formicivorus
Size: 8-10 in. (20-25 cm)
Description: A black-and-white wood-pecker with a yellowish throat, red crown and a dark goatee.
Habitat: Oak and pine forests.
Comments: Feeds on acorns and nuts. During fall harvest, it crams its food cache into tight holes to prevent theft by squirrels.

FLYCATCHERS

These compact birds characteristically sit on exposed perches and dart out to capture passing insects.

ASH-THROATED FLYCATCHER
Myiarchus cinerascens
Size: 7-9 in. (18-23 cm)
Description: A gray-brown bird with a pale yellow belly, a pale gray throat and rust-colored tail.
Habitat: Ranges from deserts to mountain woodlands.
Comments: Found throughout Arizona during summer months, it is a year-round resident near the southern border.

VERMILION FLYCATCHER
Pyrocephalus rubinus
Size: To 6 in. (15 cm)
Description: Brilliant crimson bird has a black mask and back.
Habitat: Canyons, open areas near water.
Comments: Female is dull brown with a whitish breast streaked with brown and a pink-washed belly.

BLACK PHOEBE
Sayornis nigricans
Size: 7-8 in. (18-20 cm)
Description: Black bird with a white belly. Tail has white margins.
Habitat: Deserts and woodlands near water.
Comments: Has unusual habit of wagging its tail while perching.

LARKS

Highly terrestrial, slender-billed birds found in fields with low vegetation.

HORNED LARK
Eremophila alpestris
Size: 7-8 in. (18-20 cm)
Description: Brown bird with a yellow face, dark neck and eye marks and black 'horns'.
Habitat: Open areas including fields, sagebrush plains, farmlands and parks.
Comments: Nests and feeds on the ground. Often found in flocks.

SWALLOWS

These acrobatic fliers have short bills, long, pointed wings and long tails (often forked). Their wide mouths are adapted for scooping up insects on the wing.

BARN SWALLOW
Hirundo rustica
Size: 6-8 in. (15-20 cm)
Description: Blue-black above, cinnamon below, it is easily identified in flight by its long, forked tail.
Habitat: Open woods, fields, farms and lakes.
Comments: Commonly nests in building eaves and under bridges. Summers in central and southern Arizona. The similar cliff swallow (*Petrochelidon pyrrhonota*) has a square-edged tail.

Barn

Cliff

PURPLE MARTIN
Progne subis
Size: 6-8 in. (15-20 cm)
Description: Told by blue-black plumage and dark, forked tail.
Habitat: Open woods, parks, desert.
Comments: Very abundant in cities in the fall. Often will nest in saguaro cacti. Common from April-October.

CROWS & ALLIES

These large, omnivorous birds are very common. Sexes are similar.

STELLER'S JAY
Cyanocitta stelleri
Size: 12-14 in. (30-35 cm)
Description: Distinguished at a glance by its prominent head crest and deep blue on wings, belly and tail.
Habitat: Pine and pine-oak forests.
Comments: Very gregarious, it frequents campsites and human dwellings in search of handouts.

COMMON RAVEN
Corvus corax
Size: 22-27 in. (55-68 cm)
Description: A large black bird with a heavy bill, wedge-shaped tail and shaggy head and throat.
Habitat: Highly variable, ranging from mountain forests to desert.
Comments: The similar, smaller Chihuahuan raven (*C. cryptoleucus*) is found in southeastern Arizona.

WESTERN SCRUB-JAY
Aphelocoma woodhouseii
Size: 11-13 in. (28-33 cm)
Description: A streamlined blue bird with a long bill and tail. Key field marks are white throat, incomplete blue necklace and brown back.
Habitat: Oak-chaparral, woodlands.
Comments: Common in cities and towns. Flight is undulating and short, followed by a sweeping glide.

CHICKADEES

These gregarious birds often flock together and are common at feeders.

MOUNTAIN CHICKADEE
Poecile gambeli
Size: To 5 in. (13 cm)
Description: Small grayish bird has a black crown, chin and eye stripe.
Habitat: Coniferous forests, towns.
Comments: Gregarious bird is most common in forests and mountainous areas. Call is a name-saying – *chicka-dee-dee-dee.*

NUTHATCHES

Nuthatches are stout little birds with thin, sharp bills and stumpy tails.

WHITE-BREASTED NUTHATCH
Sitta carolinensis
Size: 5-6 in. (13-15 cm)
Description: Chunky, white-faced, grayish bird with black cap, white underparts and short, sharp bill.
Habitat: Coniferous forests and pine-oak woodlands.
Comments: Creeps about on tree trunks and branches searching for insects, often descending head first.

VERDINS

Small, plump birds that often travel in small flocks.

VERDIN
Auriparus flaviceps
Size: 3-5 in. (8-13 cm)
Description: Small grayish bird with a yellow head and chestnut shoulders.
Habitat: Deserts.
Comments: Unusual nest consists of a ball of dried vegetation with a hole in the side. Feeds on insects, berries and seeds.

WRENS

This family of birds have the distinctive habit of cocking their tails in the air when perching.

CACTUS WREN
Campylorhynchus brunneicapillus
Size: 7-9 in. (18-23 cm)
Description: A large wren with a dark cap, broad white eye stripe and a spotted breast.
Habitat: Deserts, urban areas.
Comments: The largest wren in North America. Its unmusical, repetitive song of low notes – *ka-ka-ka-ka* – is a familiar desert sound.

Arizona's State Bird

MOCKINGBIRDS & THRASHERS

These long-tailed birds with long, down-turned bills often sing loudly from exposed perches.

CURVE-BILLED THRASHER
Toxostoma curvirostre
Size: 9-12 in. (23-30 cm)
Description: Gray-brown bird has a speckled breast, orange eyes and a long, strongly down-turned bill.
Habitat: Deserts, urban areas.
Comments: Often sings from atop cholla cacti in which it also nests. Two-note call is distinctive – *whit-wheet*. Very vocal January to May.

NORTHERN MOCKINGBIRD
Mimus polyglottos
Size: 9-11 in. (23-28 cm)
Description: Robin-sized, grayish bird with a downturned bill and a long tail. White wing patches are conspicuous in flight.
Habitat: Chaparral, scrubby woodlands, gardens.
Comments: Named for its habit of mimicking distinctive sounds like the calls of other birds. Often flicks its tail from side to side while perching.

THRUSHES

This group of woodland birds includes many good singers. Sexes are similar in most.

AMERICAN ROBIN
Turdus migratorius
Size: 9-11 in. (23-28 cm)
Description: Gray bird with rusty breast is familiar to most.
Habitat: Ranges from oak woodlands to coniferous forests.
Comments: Forages on the ground for insects, snails and worms. Most common in high country.

WESTERN BLUEBIRD
Sialia mexicana
Size: 6-7 in. (15-18 cm)
Description: Male is bright blue above with a rust breast and white belly. Female is brownish with dull blue wings and tail.
Habitat: Open woodlands and grasslands at mid to upper elevations.
Comments: Often seen on exposed perches when hunting for insects.

WAXWINGS

These gregarious birds are named for their red wing marks which look like waxy droplets.

CEDAR WAXWING
Bombycilla cedrorum
Size: 6-8 in. (15-20 cm)
Description: Told at a glance by its sleek, crested head, yellow belly, yellow-tipped tail and red wing marks.
Habitat: Open deciduous woods, orchards, urban areas.
Comments: Diet consists largely of berries and insects. Occurs in small flocks. Considered an irregular transient, it may be common one year and absent the next.

SHRIKES

Shrikes feed on insects, small birds and rodents. Nicknamed butcher birds, they will cache excess food taken when hunting by impaling it on tree thorns or barbed wire.

LOGGERHEAD SHRIKE
Lanius ludovicianus
Size: 8-10 in. (20-25 cm)
Description: Gray-backed bird with a black mask and a stout, hooked bill.
Habitat: Forests and open areas including deserts and grasslands.
Comments: Flight is undulating. Often seen perching atop trees and telephone wires in open country.

SILKY FLYCATCHERS

This tropical bird is found in hot, open areas.

PHAINOPEPLA
Phainopepla nitens
Size: 7-8 in. (18-20 cm)
Description: Glossy blue-black male has crested head and white wing patches (conspicuous in flight). Note red eyes.
Habitat: Desert scrub, oak woodlands, mesquite scrub.
Comments: Mistletoe berries are a favorite food.

STARLINGS

These fat-bodied, short-tailed birds are abundant in cities and towns. An introduced species.

EUROPEAN STARLING
Sturnus vulgaris
Size: 6-8 in. (15-20 cm)
Description: Chubby bird with iridescent black-purple plumage and a pointed yellow bill.
Habitat: Farms, fields, cities, deserts.
Comments: Considered a pest by many, the starling is an aggressive bird that competes with native species for food and nesting sites.

WARBLERS & ALLIES

Members of this large family are distinguished from other small birds by their thin, pointed bills.

'Myrtle' race

'Audubon's' race

YELLOW-RUMPED WARBLER
Setophaga coronata
Size: 5-6 in. (13-15 cm)
Description: Blue-gray bird with yellow rump and cap. Throat is white or yellow.
Habitat: Coniferous and mixed forests.
Comments: A relatively newly designated species, formerly the myrtle and Audubon's warblers.

YELLOW WARBLER
Dendroica petechia
Size: 4-5 in. (10-13 cm)
Description: Distinctive yellow bird with a streaked breast.
Habitat: Shrubs and thickets along river valleys, urban areas.
Comments: Song is a cheery – *sweet, sweet, sweet*. The black-masked common yellowthroat (*Geothlypis trichas*) is another familiar southwestern warbler.

Yellow

Common Yellowthroat

BLACKBIRDS & ALLIES

A diverse group of birds ranging from iridescent black birds to brightly-colored meadowlarks and orioles. All have conical, sharply-pointed bills.

BROWN-HEADED COWBIRD
Molothrus ater
Size: 6-8 in. (15-20 cm)
Description: Metallic green-black bird with brown hood and heavy bill.
Habitat: Open woods, farmlands and fields, often near domestic livestock.
Comments: Female is noted for her parasitic habit of laying eggs in the nests of other birds. While some species remove the new egg, most will raise the cowbird as their own, often at the expense of their young.

BULLOCK'S ORIOLE
Icterus bullockii
Size: 6-8 in. (15-20 cm)
Description: Distinctive black and orange bird has large white wing patches. Note black cap, chin and eye stripe.
Habitat: Open deciduous forests, ranchlands.
Comments: Builds distinctive pouch-like, woven nests that hang from tree branches. The black-headed Scott's oriole (*Icterus parisorum*) is common throughout the state in summer.

Bullock's

Scott's

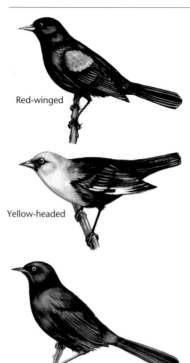

Red-winged

Yellow-headed

RED-WINGED BLACKBIRD
Agelaius phoeniceus
Size: To 10 in. (25 cm)

YELLOW-HEADED BLACKBIRD
Xanthocephalus xanthocephalus
Size: To 11 in. (28 cm)
Description: Red-winged male is black with prominent red shoulder patches. Yellow-headed male is unmistakable.
Habitat: Sloughs, marshes and wet fields.
Comments: Usually nests in reeds or tall grass near water. Gurgling songs are a familiar marsh sound.

BREWER'S BLACKBIRD
Euphagus cyanocephalus
Size: 8-10 in. (20-25 cm)
Description: Black plumage has a purplish sheen. Female is gray-brown. Eyes are yellow or white.
Habitat: Grasslands, fields, parks.
Comments: Roosts in large colonies at night.

GREAT-TAILED GRACKLE
Quiscalus mexicanus
Size: 16-17 in. (40-43 cm)
Description: Purplish-black bird has a long tail shaped like a boat's keel. Eyes are yellow. Females are brown above with buffy underparts.
Habitat: Towns, fields.
Comments: Call includes a series of whistles and harsh creaks. Very common resident of urban areas.

WESTERN MEADOWLARK
Sturnella neglecta
Size: 8-11 in. (20-28 cm)
Description: Mottled brown bird is distinguished by its bright yellow breast, white-edged tail, and dark V-shaped neckband.
Habitat: Grassy fields, meadows, wetlands.
Comments: Loud, flute-like, gurgling song is distinctive.

TANAGERS

These brightly-colored birds of tropical origin have heavy, conical, seed-cracking bills.

WESTERN TANAGER
Piranga ludoviciana
Size: 6-7 in. (15-18 cm)
Description: Yellow bird with a red head and a dark back. Females are yellowish with a gray back; some female morphs also have a gray belly and breast. All have two light wing bars.
Habitat: Coniferous and mixed woods.
Comments: Common near wooded picnic areas. Call is a slurred – *pit-ick, pit-ick.* The all-red summer tanager (*P. rubra*) is common in woodlands during summer months.

Western

Summer

FINCHES, SPARROWS & ALLIES

Members of this family have short, thick, seed-cracking bills.

NORTHERN CARDINAL
Cardinalis cardinalis
Size: 7-9 in. (18-23 cm)
Description: Crested red male is unmistakable. Crested female is yellow-brown. Note conical beak.
Habitat: Woodlands, brushy areas near water, urban areas.
Comments: A resident species common at feeders throughout the year. Both sexes sing year-round.

PYRRHULOXIA
Cardinalis sinuatus
Size: 7-8 in. (18-20 cm)
Description: Cardinal-like gray bird with a stubby, yellow beak. Red-crested male has a red stripe down the middle of its breast.
Habitat: Desert scrub.
Comments: Feeds on insects and seeds on the ground near cover.

LESSER GOLDFINCH
Carduelis psaltria
Size: 4-5 in. (10-13 cm)
Description: Male has a black cap, a black or greenish back, yellow under-parts and bold white wing marks. Duller female lacks a cap.
Habitat: Wooded groves, gardens, parks.
Comments: Often found in flocks. Song is a rapidly repeated series of ascending or descending notes.

HOUSE FINCH
Haemorhous mexicanus
Size: 5-6 in. (13-15 cm)
Description: Brown bird with a reddish forehead, streaked breast and rump.
Habitat: Deserts to oak woodlands, urban areas.
Comments: Highly social birds, they are easily attracted to feeders and nesting sites.

SONG SPARROW
Melospiza melodia
Size: 5-7 in. (13-18 cm)
Description: Distinguished by heavily-streaked breast with streaks converging to a central spot. Tail is rounded.
Habitat: Very common in bushes and woodlands near water.
Comments: Forages along the ground. Melodious song usually begins with 3-4 similar notes.

BLACK-THROATED SPARROW
Amphispiza bilineata
Size: 5-6 in. (13-15 cm)
Description: Dull colored, grayish sparrow with two light facial stripes and a long black bib.
Habitat: Deserts.
Comments: Also called the desert sparrow, it is found in habitats with cacti and mesquite. Extremely drought tolerant, it drinks less water than any other seed-eating bird.

SPOTTED TOWHEE
Pipilo maculatus
Size: 7-9 in. (18-23 cm)
Description: Told by its black hood, rust sides, white belly and red eyes. Female is brown where the male is black.
Habitat: Woodlands and urban areas.
Comments: Formerly known as the rufous-sided towhee. Its dull-brown cousin, the canyon towhee (*Melozone fuscus*), is also common in woods and gardens.

Spotted

Canyon

DARK-EYED JUNCO
Junco hyemalis
Size: 5-7 in. (13-18 cm)
Description: Key field marks are dark head, whitish bill, white belly and white-edged tail. Has gray sides and a gray back or a black head and a brown back.
Habitat: Coniferous and mixed woods, gardens, parks.
Comments: Gregarious and easily attracted to feeders. A relatively newly designated species, formerly the slate-colored junco, Oregon junco, gray-headed Junco and white-winged junco.

'Slate-colored' race

'Oregon' race

WEAVER FINCHES

These sparrow-like birds were introduced to North America in 1850, and are now widespread throughout the continent.

HOUSE SPARROW
Passer domesticus
Size: 5-6 in. (13-15 cm)
Description: Black throat and brown nape of male are key field marks. Females and young are dull brown with a light eye stripe.
Habitat: Suburbs, cities, farmlands.
Comments: These gregarious, social birds gather in large flocks between breeding seasons.

WHAT ARE REPTILES & AMPHIBIANS?

Reptiles and amphibians represent a diverse array of water- and land-dwelling animals.

REPTILES

Reptiles can generally be described as scaly-skinned, terrestrial creatures that breathe through lungs. The majority reproduce by laying eggs on land; in some, the eggs develop inside the mother who later gives birth to live young. Contrary to popular belief, very few are harmful to man. All are valuable in controlling rodent and insect populations.

The most common types of Arizona reptiles are turtles, lizards and snakes.

AMPHIBIANS

Amphibians are smooth-skinned, limbed vertebrates that live in moist habitats and breathe through either lungs, skin, gills or a combination of all three. While they spend much of their lives on land, they still depend on a watery environment to complete their life cycle. Most reproduce by laying eggs in or near water. The young hatch as swimming larvae, tadpoles, for example, that breathe through gills. After a short developmental period the larvae metamorphose into young adults with lungs and legs.

The most common types of Arizona amphibians are salamanders, frogs and toads.

HOW TO IDENTIFY REPTILES & AMPHIBIANS

Reptiles are secretive but can be observed if you know where to look. Turtles are found on the edges of ponds and lakes and often sun themselves on rocks and logs. Lizards sun themselves in habitats ranging from open deserts to suburban back yards and are the most conspicuous reptiles. The best time to look for snakes is in the early morning or late afternoon when it's not too hot. They can be found in deserts, canyons and along trails and watercourses. They often rest during the day under logs and rocks, so one should exercise care when moving such objects.

Of the amphibians, frogs and toads are probably the easiest to observe since they loudly announce their presence during breeding season. Frogs are found in wet areas on or near the water. Toads are more terrestrial and may be found far from water, especially during the day. Salamanders are more secretive and rarely venture out of their cool, moist habitats.

Caution – When seeking reptiles, watch where you step. Many snakes are well-camouflaged and can be sluggish in the morning or after eating. Also, be careful where you put your hands. Do not put hands in places you can't see into. Turn over rocks and logs with a stick or tool.

TURTLES

Turtles are easily distinguished by their large bony shells, which serve to protect them from predators. They are most active in spring during mating season. Most are omnivores and eat a wide variety of plant and animal matter.

DESERT TORTOISE
Gopherus agassizii
Size: 10-15 in. (25-38 cm)
Description: Distinguished by its high-domed, deeply ridged shell and thick, stumpy legs.
Habitat: Dry, sandy areas.
Comments: Typically feeds at dawn and dusk and rests in a shallow burrow during the day.

SONORAN MUD TURTLE
Kinosternon sonoriense
Size: 3-6 in. (8-15 cm)
Description: Small, flat-shelled brown turtle with nipple-like bumps on its throat.
Habitat: Near water in desert and woodland habitats in southern Arizona.
Comments: Like all mud turtles, it has a strong, musky odor.

POND SLIDER
Trachemys scripta
Size: 5-12 in. (13-30 cm)
Description: Distinguished by its round, yellow-marked shell and colored blotches (red, orange or yellow) behind its eyes.
Habitat: Ponds, waterways, ditches.
Comments: The common pet store turtle. Many have been introduced and may outnumber native turtles in some areas.

DESERT BOX TURTLE
Terrapene ornata luteola
Size: 4-6 in. (10-15 cm)
Description: Distinguished by its high, domed shell. Brown and yellow lines radiate from spots on each side.
Habitat: Prairies, sandy areas, open woodlands in southern Arizona.
Comments: Eats primarily insects. Many are killed crossing roads following rainstorms.

LIZARDS

Lizards are scaly-skinned animals that usually have 4 legs and a tail, movable eyelids, visible ear openings, claws and toothed jaws. A few species are legless and superficially resemble snakes. Lizards represent the largest group of living reptiles and range in size from tiny skinks to the giant 10-foot-long monitor lizards of Indonesia. Of the more than 3,000 species found worldwide, 95 occur in the U.S.

WESTERN BANDED GECKO
Coleonyx variegatus
Size: 3-6 in. (8-15 cm)
Description: Tan-colored, banded lizard with large eyes and prominent eyelids. Banding pattern is variable among three Arizona subspecies.
Habitat: Deserts and foothills in southern Arizona.
Comments: Primarily nocturnal, it is often spotted at night along desert roads.

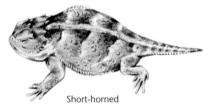

Short-horned

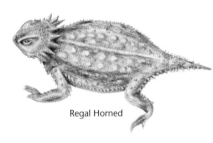

Regal Horned

SHORT-HORNED LIZARD
Phrynosoma douglassi
Size: 3-6 in. (8-15 cm)
Description: Brown-gray lizard's head is covered with stubby spines; trunk is fringed by pointed scales.
Habitat: Rocky, sandy and forested areas.
Comments: Feeds primarily on ants and can be spotted in the vicinity of ant hills. Horned lizards are called horned toads by some. The similar regal horned lizard (*P. solare*) is gray-brown and has prominent head spines. When caught, it becomes flat and rigid and will flop on its back. May squirt blood from its eyes in defense.

DESERT IGUANA
Dipsosaurus dorsalis
Size: 10-16 in. (25-40 cm)
Description: Pale, round-bodied lizard with a smallish head and long tail. Tail is encircled by rows of dark spots.
Habitat: Deserts, creosote scrub.
Comments: Active during the day, it feeds exclusively on plants.

SIDE-BLOTCHED LIZARD
Uta stansburiana
Size: 4-6 in. (10-15 cm)
Description: Small brownish lizard with a blotched back and sides. Several variants exist, most of which have a prominent dark spot behind each front leg.
Habitat: Arid and semi-arid regions.
Comments: Primarily ground-dwelling, it feeds on insects during the day.

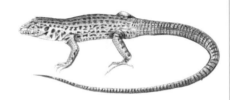

WESTERN WHIPTAIL
Aspidoscelis tigris
Size: To 12 in. (30 cm)
Description: A gray, yellowish or brown lizard with bars, spots or a web of lines on its back and sides. Note its long tail.
Habitat: Deserts and open forests.
Comments: Active during the day and often encountered. Moves in jerky steps, with its head darting side-to-side.

WESTERN FENCE LIZARD
Sceloporus occidentalis
Size: 6-9 in. (15-23 cm)
Description: Spiny-scaled, brown-green or black lizard with blue patches on neck, sides and belly.
Habitat: Rocky areas, mixed forests, near buildings and fences.
Comments: Active during the day, it is often encountered. Will display blue undersides to attract females or defend territory.

COLLARED LIZARD
Crotaphytus collaris
Size: 9-14 in. (23-35 cm)
Description: Greenish, long-tailed lizard with two dark collar markings.
Habitat: Rocky areas in deserts, foothills and forests.
Comments: It flees danger by running swiftly on its hind legs. Will bite readily if handled.

CHUCKWALLA
Sauromalus obesus
Size: 10-17 in. (25-43 cm)
Description: Large lizard with potbelly and fat tail. Note loose folds of skin on the neck and back. Young have a yellow and black-banded tail.
Habitat: Deserts and rocky areas.
Comments: Noted for its unusual defensive behavior; when disturbed, it darts between rock crevices and wedges itself in by inflating its body.

ZEBRA-TAILED LIZARD
Callisaurus draconoides
Size: To 9 in. (23 cm)
Description: Gray-brown lizard has a prominently banded tail. Note folds of skin on throat. Underside of tail is white with black bands.
Habitat: Hard-packed desert soils.
Comments: A fast-moving lizard that curls its tail over its back when running.

ARIZONA (GILBERT'S) SKINK
Eumeces gilberti
Size: To 13 in. (33 cm)
Description: Chubby yellow-brown lizard has 4 light back stripes. Young are also striped and have a yellowish tail.
Habitat: Open forests, near waterways.
Comments: Active during the day, it is often seen sunning itself or foraging for food in grassy areas.

GILA MONSTER
Heloderma suspectum
Size: 18-24 in. (45-60 cm)
Description: Heavy-bodied lizard with blotched, bead-like skin in contrasting pattern of red, black or yellow.
Habitat: Sandy or rocky soils in desert.
Comments: The only venomous lizard in the U.S., it should be treated with caution if encountered. Name is pronounced *HEE-la* monster.

SNAKES

Snakes are limbless reptiles with dry, scaly skin, toothed jaws, no ear openings or eyelids and a single row of belly scales. They move by contracting their muscles in waves and undulating over the ground. All are carnivorous and swallow their prey whole. They flick their tongues in and out constantly to 'taste' and 'smell' the air around them. Most continue to grow in length during their life and shed their outer skin periodically. The vast majority are harmless to humans.

COMMON KINGSNAKE
Lampropeltis getulus
Size: 3-7 ft. (.9-2.1 m)
Description: Told by pattern of alternating dark and light rings along body. An all-black variant is found in southern Arizona.
Habitat: Deserts, forests, rocky areas.
Comments: Active in mornings and afternoons, it hunts at night during hot weather. Diet consists of small mammals, rodents, lizards and snakes (including rattlers!).

BLACK-NECKED GARTER SNAKE
Thamnophis cyrtopsis
Size: 20-43 in. (50-109 cm)
Description: Olive to brown snake with two prominent black neck blotches and a yellow to orange back stripe.
Habitat: Near water in desert flats, forests and canyons.
Comments: Active during the day, it is frequently observed sunning itself on rocks near water in the morning. A good swimmer, it feeds primarily on amphibians and invertebrates.

GLOSSY SNAKE
Arizona elegans
Size: To 6 ft. (1.8 m)
Description: Cream to brownish snake has dark blotches down its back and sides that are edged in black. Scales are smooth and glossy.
Habitat: Deserts, grasslands, woodlands.
Comments: Is also called the faded snake owing to its bleached coloration. Feeds primarily on lizards.

GOPHER SNAKE
Pituophis melanoleucus
Size: 3-8 ft. (.9-2.4 m)
Description: Large, yellow-cream snake with dark blotches on its back and sides.
Habitat: Deserts, forests.
Comments: Though non-venomous, it imitates a rattlesnake when threatened by coiling up, hissing loudly, vibrating its tail and striking out at its aggressor. Eats primarily small rodents and is valued for pest control.

POISONOUS SNAKES

WESTERN RATTLESNAKE
Crotalus viridis
Size: 1-5 ft. (30-150 cm)
Description: A darkly-blotched, greenish-brown snake with a flat triangular head, defined neck and tail rattle.
Habitat: Grasslands, brushy areas and woodlands from sea level to 11,000 ft. (3,350 m).
Comments: A pit viper, it has heat sensing areas between its eyes and nostrils which help it detect prey. Enlarged front fangs have hollow canals which inject venom into prey when it strikes. Eats mostly rodents.

ARIZONA RIDGE-NOSED RATTLESNAKE
Crotalus willardi
Size: 1-2 ft. (30-60 cm)
Description: Gray, brown or reddish snake with light flash marks on head. Upper snout has a prominent ridge.
Habitat: Pine-oak woodlands in extreme southeast Arizona.
Comments: Protected species is found in the Santa Rita and Huachuca mountains in southern Arizona.

Arizona's State Reptile

WESTERN DIAMOND-BACK RATTLESNAKE
Crotalus atrox
Size: 3-7 ft. (.9-2.1 m)
Description: A thick-bodied grayish snake with brown diamond-like blotches down its back. Also has distinct black-and-white bands on its tail preceding the rattle.
Habitat: Variable, from the desert to the mountains.
Comments: One of the most dangerous North American snakes, its bite can be fatal to humans. Like all rattlesnakes, it is normally non-aggressive to humans; most bite only when threatened.

BLACK-TAILED RATTLESNAKE
Crotalus molossus
Size: 28-50 in. (70-125 cm)
Description: Greenish to grayish snake has light-centered cross-bands down its back. Tail is black before the rattle.
Habitat: Mountainous areas.
Comments: Nocturnal snake is considered to be non-aggressive.

ARIZONA CORAL SNAKE
Micruroides euryxanthus
Size: To 21 in. (53 cm)
Description: Unmistakable black, yellow and red banded snake with a black snout. Note how red and yellow bands touch one another.
Habitat: Upland deserts and mountainous areas.
Comments: An extremely poisonous snake with paralyzing venom. There are similar red and black banded snakes that are harmless mimics. The rhyme to remember is "red on yellow can kill a fellow".

FROGS & TOADS

Frogs and toads are squat amphibians common near ponds and lakes. All have large heads, large eyes, long hind legs and long, sticky tongues that they use to catch insects. Most have well-developed ears and strong voices. Only males are vocal.

Frogs have smooth skin, slim waists and many have prominent dorsal ridges. In most, the male initiates mating by calling for females. When he finds a mate, he clasps her in water and fertilizes the eggs as they are laid. The eggs initially hatch into fish-like tadpoles that breathe through gills and feed on vegetation. They later transform into young adults with limbs and lungs.

Toads can be distinguished from frogs by their dry, warty skin and prominent glands behind their eyes (parotoids). Some also have swellings between their eyes (bosses). When handled roughly by would-be predators, the warts and glands secrete a poisonous substance that makes the toads extremely unpalatable. Contrary to popular belief, handling toads does not cause warts.

Arizona's State Amphibian

ARIZONA TREEFROG
Hyla eximia
Size: 1-2 in. (3-5 cm)
Description: Small green frog with toe pads and a dark eye stripe extending beyond the shoulder.
Habitat: Forest meadows at elevations above 5,000 ft. (1,524 m).
Comments: Most active during summer breeding season. Voice is a monotone clacking.

CANYON TREEFROG
Hyla arenicolor
Size: 1-2 in. (3-5 cm)
Description: Small green-brown frog that lacks an eye stripe and has prominent toe pads.
Habitat: Ponds, streams and lakes in woodlands and canyons.
Comments: Call is an explosive whirring note that lasts up to 3 seconds. Breeds in early summer.

BULLFROG
Lithobates catesbeiana
Size: 4-8 in. (10-20 cm)
Description: Large green-brown frog with large ear openings.
Habitat: Ponds and lakes with ample vegetation.
Comments: Nocturnal; it is often seen along shorelines. Voice is a deep-pitched – *jug-o-rum*. An introduced species.

NORTHERN LEOPARD FROG
Rana pipiens
Size: To 5 in. (13 cm)
Description: Brown to green frog has light-edged dark spots. Snout is relatively pointed. A ridge of skin runs from behind the eye to the groin.
Habitat: Marshes, waterways, wet meadows.
Comments: Call is a rattling snore. Primarily nocturnal.

RED-SPOTTED TOAD
Bufo punctatus
Size: 1-3 in. (3-8 cm)
Description: Brown-gray, flat-bodied toad with reddish warts.
Habitat: Deserts, grasslands, canyons.
Comments: Primarily nocturnal, it may be active in daylight hours during its breeding season (April-September).

WESTERN SPADEFOOT TOAD
Scaphiopus hammondi
Size: 1-3 in. (3-8 cm)
Description: Brown-gray-green toad covered with dark blotches. Skin has small bumps that are tipped in red or orange. Glossy, black wedge-shaped spade on each hind foot is used to excavate burrows.
Habitat: Desert lowlands.
Comments: Lives in deep burrows and is primarily nocturnal. Rolling call resembles a cat's purr.

WHAT ARE FISHES?

Fishes are cold-blooded vertebrates that live in water and breathe dissolved oxygen through organs called gills. They are generally characterized by their size, shape, feeding habits, and water temperature preference. Most live in either saltwater or freshwater, though a few species divide their lives between the two (these are referred to as anadromous fishes).

All fishes have streamlined bodies covered in scales, and swim by flexing their bodies from side to side. Their fins help to steer while swimming and can also act as brakes. Many species possess an internal air bladder which acts as a depth regulator. By secreting gases into the bladder or absorbing gases from it, they are able to control the depth at which they swim.

Most fish reproduce by laying eggs freely in the water. In many, the male discharges sperm over the eggs as they are laid by the female. Depending on the species, eggs may float, sink, become attached to vegetation, or be buried.

HOW TO IDENTIFY FISHES

First, note the size, shape and color of the fish. Are there any distinguishing field marks like the double dorsal fins of the basses or the downturned lips of the suckers? Is the body thin or torpedo-shaped? Note the orientation and placement of fins on the body. Consult the text to confirm identification.

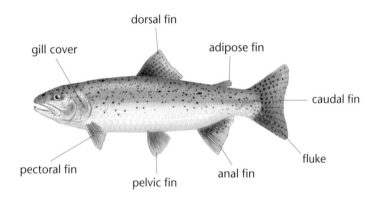

TROUT & ALLIES

This diverse group includes many popular sport fishes. Most have robust bodies, square caudal fins, an adipose fin and strong teeth.

BROOK TROUT
Salvelinus fontinalis
Size: To 21 in. (53 cm)
Description: Colorful greenish fish with blue-haloed, red side spots and wavy light lines on back and dorsal fin. Lower fins are reddish.
Habitat: Clear, freshwater streams and rivers; some are anadromous.
Comments: An introduced sport fish weighing up to 14 lbs. (6.3 kg).

RAINBOW TROUT
Oncorhynchus mykiss
Size: To 2 ft. (60 cm)
Description: A dark-spotted fish named for the distinctive reddish band running down its side. Band is most prominent during spring spawning.
Habitat: Abundant in cold streams, reservoirs and lakes.
Comments: Introduced to lakes and ponds throughout Arizona.

BROWN TROUT
Salmo trutta
Size: To 40 in. (1 m)
Description: Golden-brown fish covered with large brown or black spots surrounded by light halos. Red or orange spots are also evident on the sides of the fish.
Habitat: Cool streams and lakes.
Comments: An introduced species renowned for its wariness.

APACHE TROUT
Oncorhynchus apache
Size: To 19 in. (48 cm)
Description: A yellowish, dark-spotted trout. Two dark spots on either side of pupil form a line through the eye.
Habitat: Native to the Upper Salt and Little Colorado river systems, it has been introduced to other lakes and streams.
Comments: Almost eradicated by introduced trout, it has been saved by intensive habitat reconstruction.

Arizona's State Fish

MINNOWS & ALLIES

These fishes can be distinguished from similar species by their lack of an adipose fin and toothless jaws. Lips are typically thin and tail is well-forked.

SPECKLED DACE
Rhinichthys osculus
Size: To 4 in. (10 cm)
Description: Highly variable, it is usually a dusky gray-olive color with a black-speckled body and distinct side stripe.
Habitat: Pools, streams, rivers.
Comments: There are numerous subspecies of this widespread, native minnow.

LONGFIN DACE
Agosia chrysogaster
Size: To 3.5 in. (9 cm)
Description: Olive-gray above, it has a dark side stripe ending in a spot near the tail. Female has elongated lower lobe on anal fin.
Habitat: Pools, streams, rivers.
Comments: Eats insects, algae and small invertebrates.

SPIKEDACE
Meda fulgida
Size: To 3 in. (8 cm)
Description: A slender, silvery, scaleless fish, often with black specks on its sides. Breeding male has a yellowish head.
Habitat: Sandy and rocky runs in the Gila and Verde river systems.
Comments: Considered a threatened species, it has been displaced in many areas by introduced fish like the red shiner.

GOLDFISH
Carassius auratus
Size: To 16 in. (40 cm)
Description: Thick gray-brown fish with large scales and a long dorsal fin.
Habitat: Sluggish streams, muddy ponds, sloughs.
Comments: Native to China, they are tolerant of warm and polluted waters. Domesticated goldfish are the more familiar orange color.

GOLDEN SHINER
Notemigonus crysoleucas
Size: To 12 in. (30 cm)
Description: Deep-bodied, narrow fish with silver-olive sides and light-colored fins. A dark side stripe is often visible.
Habitat: Vegetated pools, streams, rivers and ponds.
Comments: Common bait fish often found in schools near the shore. A non-native species introduced throughout Arizona.

RED SHINER
Notropis lutrensis
Size: To 3.5 in. (9 cm)
Description: Deep-bodied, silvery-blue fish with a rounded snout and a blue triangular bar behind the head. Breeding male has reddish fins.
Habitat: Streams and pools.
Comments: Common in turbid waters.

FATHEAD MINNOW
Pimephales promelas
Size: To 4 in. (10 cm)
Description: Stout, brassy fish with a blunt nose. Breeding male has a black head, two light side bars and a number of bumps on its snout.
Habitat: Muddy and clear pools, creeks, small rivers.
Comments: A common introduced baitfish.

COMMON CARP
Cyprinus carpio
Size: To 30 in. (75 cm)
Description: A large-scaled, deep-bodied olive fish, it is identified by its long dorsal fin, mouth barbels (whiskers) and forked, orangish tail. Dorsal fin has a single spine.
Habitat: Found in clear and turbid streams, ponds and sloughs. Prefers warm water.
Comments: Asian species has been introduced throughout Arizona.

LIVEBEARERS

Livebearers are fertilized internally and give birth to live young.

MOSQUITOFISH
Gambusia affinis
Size: To 2.5 in. (6 cm)
Description: Gray to brownish fish with bluish sides. Has dusky teardrop and 1-3 rows of dark spots on dorsal fin and tail.
Habitat: Ponds, lakes, slow-moving streams.
Comments: Feeds on mosquito larvae and has been widely introduced throughout Arizona.

GILA TOPMINNOW
Poeciliopsis occidentalis
Size: To 2 in. (5 cm)
Description: Female is olive-brown with a dark side stripe. Male is black with orange at the base of its fins.
Habitat: Pools, vegetated springs, backwaters of creeks, small rivers.
Comments: Once very common, this native fish is now considered an endangered species. Plans to help it recover include removing competitors like mosquitofish from certain areas.

CICHLIDS

Popular aquarium fishes noted for their elaborate breeding behaviors.

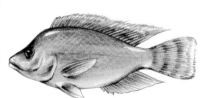

MOZAMBIQUE TILAPIA
Oreochromis mossambica
Size: To 15 in. (38 cm)
Description: Silvery gray-green fish with long dorsal and anal fins and a pronounced snout. Breeding males are blackish.
Habitat: Warm, weedy ponds, streams, canals.
Comments: Feeds on aquatic weeds and has been widely introduced to control weed growth. The spotted tilapia (*Tilapia mariae*) is also found in Arizona.

CATFISHES

Over 45 species of this large family of bottomfeeders are found in North America.

BLACK BULLHEAD
Ameiurus melas
Size: To 2 ft. (60 cm)
Description: Torpedo-shaped olive-black fish with a rounded anal fin and dark chin barbels.
Habitat: Lakes, reservoirs, muddy streams, backwaters.
Comments: Highly tolerant of polluted, turbid water, it has been widely introduced.

FLATHEAD CATFISH
Pylodictis olivaris
Size: To 53 in. (1.38 m)
Description: This dark, mottled fish is distinguished by its wide, flat head, and jutting lower jaw. The top lobe of its caudal fin is light colored.
Habitat: Lakes, creeks and reservoirs.
Comments: Popular sport and food fish is often found in nearshore waters under some form of cover.

CHANNEL CATFISH
Ictalurus punctatus
Size: To 4 ft. (1.2 m)
Description: Olive to blue-gray catfish has dark spots on its back and sides and a rounded anal fin.
Habitat: Deep pools in rivers.
Comments: The most widely introduced catfish in Arizona.

BLUE CATFISH
Ictalurus furcatus
Size: To 5.5 ft. (1.7 m)
Description: Body is blue to blue-gray above and white below. Large anal fin has a straight edge.
Habitat: Large waterways with sandy or rocky bottoms.
Comments: One of the largest North American freshwater fishes, it is a prized table fish.

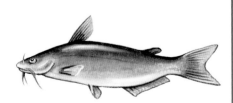

PERCH ORDER

This general category includes members of the largest order of bony fishes, perciformes. All have dorsal and anal fins that possess spines. Because of this, they are often referred to as spiny-rayed fishes.

LARGEMOUTH BASS
Micropterus salmoides
Size: To 38 in. (95 cm)
Description: Greenish, mottled fish with a dark, often blotched, side stripe. Has a large mouth with the upper jaw extending past the eye.
Habitat: Quiet, vegetated lakes, ponds and rivers.
Comments: Popular introduced sport fish renowned for its fighting ability.

SMALLMOUTH BASS
Micropterus dolomieui
Size: To 27 in. (68 cm)
Description: Similar to the largemouth, it has blotched sides and its jaw margin does not extend beyond the eye.
Habitat: Cool streams, lakes, reservoirs.
Comments: Prefers cooler, deeper water than the largemouth bass.

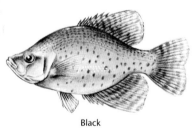

Black

BLACK CRAPPIE
Pomoxis nigromaculatus
Size: To 16 in. (40 cm)
Description: Gray-green, mottled fish with a hunched back. Dorsal fin is set well back and has 7-8 spines on its leading edge.
Habitat: Quiet, clear lakes, ponds and rivers.
Comments: Another non-native species that has been widely intro-duced in Arizona, the white crappie (*P. annularis*), has 6 spines in its first dorsal fin.

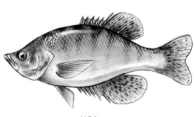

White

BLUEGILL
Lepomis macrochirus
Size: To 16 in. (40 cm)
Description: Flattened fish with long pectoral fins and a dark-spotted dorsal fin. Side bars are usually visible. Body color ranges from blue to yellow.
Habitat: Quiet, vegetated lakes, ponds and rivers.
Comments: One of the most popular panfishes in the country.

STRIPED BASS
Morone saxatilis
Size: To 6 ft. (1.8 m)
Description: Olive to blue-gray fish with 6-9 dark side stripes.
Habitat: Lakes, reservoirs.
Comments: A saltwater fish that spawns in freshwater, it has been successfully introduced to a number of lakes in Arizona.

YELLOW PERCH
Perca flavescens
Size: To 16 in. (40 cm)
Description: Golden to brown fish with 6-9 dark side patches (saddles). Note black blotching at back of first dorsal fin.
Habitat: Clear streams, ponds and lakes.
Comments: Stocked in a number of lakes, it is a popular sport and food fish.

WALLEYE
Sander vitreus
Size: To 40 in. (1 m)
Description: Slender, dark fish with large fins, a huge mouth and a white spot on the bottom of its tail fin. Dark blotching is evident at the rear of the first dorsal fin.
Habitat: Deep water in streams, lakes and reservoirs.
Comments: Named for its opaque, glassy eyes.

WHAT ARE INVERTEBRATES?

This broad classification includes all forms of animal life that lack backbones. It includes more than a million distinct species, the majority of which are insects. (Vertebrates, by comparison, comprise a mere 50,000 species.)

The major groups of invertebrates include single-celled protozoans, sponges, coelenterates, flatworms, roundworms, segmented worms, starfish and allies, mollusks, crustaceans, spiders and allies, and insects.

Following are a few notable Arizona species.

TIGER BEETLE
Cicindela spp.
Size: To .75 in. (2 cm)
Description: Distinguished by metallic green-blue-bronze body.
Habitat: Open areas.
Comments: Fast runners, they take to flight readily when disturbed. Feed on a variety of insects and spiders.

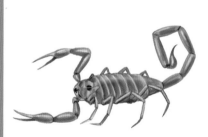

BARK SCORPION
Centruroides exilicauda
Size: To 3 in. (8 cm)
Description: Yellowish crab-like creature with pincers and a slender, stinger-tipped tail.
Habitat: In desert under ground litter or stones.
Comments: The most venomous of a number of scorpions found in the desert region. Sting is dangerous to humans so avoid it at all costs. *See section on desert awareness.*

♀

BLACK WIDOW SPIDER
Latrodectus mactans
Size: To .5 in. (1.3 cm)
Description: Shiny black spider. The female has a red hourglass-shaped figure on its abdomen.
Habitat: Variable, in buildings.
Comments: Female is poisonous and will bite if provoked.

TERMITES
Order Isoptera
Size: To .5 in. (1.3 cm)
Description: Pale-colored, soft bodied insects, often called white ants. Body shape is determined by social role it has in the colony.
Habitat: Deserts, dry woods.
Comments: Most species eat wood and frequently infest wood-framed houses. Termites and ants are among the most abundant Arizona insects.

GRAND WESTERN CICADA
Tibicen dorsata
Size: To 1.5 in. (4 cm)
Description: Square-headed, brown-black to greenish insect with large, brownish wings.
Habitat: Mixed woods.
Comments: More often heard than seen, the males' whining song can be heard on summer nights. Spends most of its time in trees.

DESERT MILLIPEDE
Orthoporous ornatus
Size: To 6 in. (15 cm)
Description: Slender, segmented insect has two pairs of legs per segment. Color is brown to yellowish.
Habitat: Deserts.
Comments: Common in spring when rains cause it to vacate its burrows. The other large segmented insect, the giant desert centipede (*Scolopendra heros*) has about 20 segments with one pair of legs per segment.

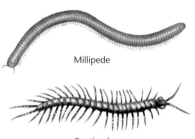

Millipede

Centipede

DESERT TARANTULA
Aphonopelma chalcodes
Size: To 3 in. (8 cm)
Description: Large, hairy, heavy-bodied spider. Color is brown to gray.
Habitat: Deserts.
Comments: Primarily nocturnal, it is often spotted at dusk and dawn when feeding or seeking a mate. Hides in burrows during the day.

WHAT ARE TREES & SHRUBS?

TREES

Trees can be broadly defined as perennial woody plants at least 16 ft. (5 m) tall with a single stem and a well-developed crown of branches, twigs and leaves. Most are long-lived plants and range in age from 40-50 years for smaller deciduous trees to several hundred years for many of the conifers.

A tree's size and shape is largely determined by its genetic makeup, but growth is also affected by environmental factors such as moisture, light and competition from other species. Trees growing in crowded stands will often only support compact crowns due to the competition for light. Some species at high altitudes grow gnarled and twisted as a result of exposure to high winds.

| Pine | Juniper | Willow | Oak | Cottonwood |

SHRUBS

Shrubs are perennial woody plants normally less than 16 ft. (5 m) tall that support a crown of branches, twigs and leaves. Unlike trees, they are anchored to the ground by several stems rather than a single trunk. Most are fast-growing and provide an important source of food and shelter for wildlife.

N.B. – *Some shrubs that are most conspicuous when in bloom are included in the following section on flowering plants.*

CACTI

This category includes a diverse array of desert and subtropical plants including palms, yuccas and cacti. Many are widely cultivated and common in urban settings. Palms and yuccas have leaves, whereas cacti have spines instead of leaves. Most are evergreen.

HOW TO IDENTIFY TREES AND SHRUBS

First, note its size and shape. Does it have one or several 'trunks.' Examine the size, color, and shape of the leaves and how they are arranged on the twigs. Are they opposite or alternate? Simple or compound? Hairy or smooth? Are flowers or fruits visible on branches or on the ground? Once you've collected as much information as you can, consult the illustrations and text to confirm your sighting.

SIMPLE LEAF SHAPES

| Elliptical | Heart-shaped | Rounded | Oval | Lobed | Lance-shaped |

COMPOUND LEAVES

LEAF ARRANGEMENTS

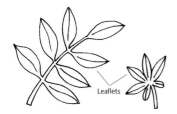

Leaflets

| Alternate | Opposite | Whorled |

COMMON FRUITS

Drupe
junipers, cherries, dogwoods, hollies

Pome
apples, plums, yuccas, pears

Nut
walnuts, pecans, hickories

Berry-like
blackberries, oranges, tomatoes

Winged Seed
dandelions, milkweeds, poplars, cottonwoods

Samara
maples, ashes, hophornbeams, elms

Acorn
oaks

Pod
peas, mesquites, locusts

PINES

Most have long, needle-like leaves that grow grouped in bundles of 2-5. Male and female cones usually occur on the same tree.

PONDEROSA PINE
Pinus ponderosa
Size: 50-130 ft. (15-40 m)
Description: Stout, stiff needles 5-8 in. (13-20 cm) long and grouped in bundles of 2-3. Oval cones have scales that terminate in sharp prickles.
Habitat: Widespread in mountain regions, often in pure stands.
Comments: Central Arizona has the country's largest unbroken stand of ponderosa pines.

BRISTLECONE PINE
Pinus aristata
Size: 20-40 ft. (6-12 m)
Description: Tree with needles arranged into tight bundles of 5 that grow curved around the twig. Purplish cones bristle with stiff, curved prickles.
Habitat: Dry, rocky exposed slopes.
Comments: The oldest living trees on earth, they are found in the San Francisco Peaks at elevations above 8,000 ft. (2,500 m).

COLORADO PINYON PINE
Pinus edulis
Size: 15-45 ft. (4.5-13.5 m)
Description: Small, often shrubby, pine with spreading, rounded branches. Stiff needles grow in 2's along twigs. Short-stalked, rounded cones produce large seeds.
Habitat: Dry, gravelly and rocky soils.
Comments: Common in northern and eastern Arizona, it is an important food source for jays, turkeys, bears, squirrels and deer. Common on the South Rim of the Grand Canyon.

LIMBER PINE
Pinus flexilis
Size: 30-125 ft. (9-38 m)
Description: Needles occur in stiff bundles of 5 and are clustered near the ends of branches. Large cones are up to 8 in. (20 cm) long.
Habitat: Mountain forests above 6,000 ft. (1828 m).
Comments: Is named for its flexible, tough twigs. Grows prostrate in exposed locations.

FIRS

Firs are medium-sized evergreens with dense, symmetrical crowns. Cones grow upright from branches and disintegrate when seeds are ripe. After the cone scales are shed, a central, candle-like stalk remains on the branch.

WHITE FIR
Abies concolor
Size: 100-160 ft. (30-49 m)
Description: Flexible needles are flat and blunt-tipped and grow to the sides or curve upward. Cylindrical cones are green, purple or yellow and up to 5 in. (13 cm) long.
Habitat: Moist soils in mountains.
Comments: An important food source for deer, grouse, porcupines, rodents and birds.

DOUGLAS-FIRS

Larger than true firs, Douglas-firs are easily identified by their shaggy cones.

DOUGLAS-FIR
Pseudotsuga menziesii
Size: 100-250 ft. (30-76 m)
Description: Flexible needles grow along twigs that terminate in red buds. Cones are distinguished at a glance by the 3-pointed bracts protruding between scales. Branches often droop.
Habitat: Moist, well-drained soils.
Comments: One of the tallest and most important timber trees in the U.S.

SPRUCES

Relatively large evergreens found in the mountains, they are easily distinguished by their four-sided needles that grow from woody pegs along the branches. It is much easier to roll a spruce needle between your fingers than the two-sided needles of other evergreens.

ENGELMANN SPRUCE
Picea engelmannii
Size: 80-115 ft. (24-35 m)
Description: Long barren trunk typically supports a compact conical crown of branches. Needles have sharp tips and exude a pungent odor when crushed. Ragged cones (2 in./5 cm long) are pendant and often grow in clusters.
Habitat: Moist soils in the mountains.
Comments: Found at elevations above 8,500 ft. (2,600 m).

BLUE SPRUCE
Picea pungens
Size: 65-115 ft. (20-35 m)
Description: Diamond shaped needles are very prickly. Cones up to (4 in./10 cm long) have ragged scales.
Habitat: Subalpine coniferous forests.
Comments: Found in northern and Eastern Arizona at elevations above 6,000 ft. (1828 m).

CYPRESSES & ALLIES

All have scaly or awl-shaped leaves which are tightly bunched together on twigs. The heavily-weighted twigs usually droop at their tips and give the plants a relaxed profile.

ARIZONA CYPRESS
Cupressus arizonica
Size: 16-80 ft. (4.8-24 m)
Description: Tree with scale-like leaves and a dense conical crown. Red-brown bark has vertical scars. Woody cones (1 in./3 cm long) are rounded and divided into sections.
Habitat: Rocky hillsides and canyons.
Comments: The country's most wide-spread true cypress, it ranges between California and Texas.

UTAH JUNIPER
Juniperus osteosperma
Size: To 26 ft. (8 m)
Description: Shrub or small tree with twisted trunk(s) and slim, ascending branches forming an irregular crown. Leaves are small and scale-like. Red-brown, berry-like cones are fibrous.
Habitat: Rocky hillsides and canyons.
Comments: Often associated with pinyon pines and oneseed juniper.

ROCKY MOUNTAIN JUNIPER
Juniperus scopulorum
Size: 15-50 ft. (4.5-15 m)
Description: Shrub or small tree. Leaves are small and scale-like. Juicy, bluish berries normally contain 2-3 seeds.
Habitat: Dry slopes, canyons.
Comments: Aromatic wood is often used to construct cedar chests. Specimens of this hardy plant live up to 1,500 years.

WILLOWS & ALLIES

Most have narrow, finely-toothed leaves which grow alternately along twigs. Flowers often appear in spring before the leaves along semi-erect catkins. After pollination, flowers are succeeded by small pods. When ripe, these pods burst open and shed numerous cottony seeds in the wind.

ARROYO WILLOW
Salix lasiolepis
Size: 16-40 ft. (4.8-12 m)
Description: Thicket-forming shrub or small tree with an irregular crown of erect branches. Lance-shaped, long leaves are finely-toothed. Flowers appear before the leaves in spring.
Habitat: Wet soils along arroyos and streams.
Comments: Noted for their extensive root systems, willows are often instrumental in preventing soil erosion along stream banks.

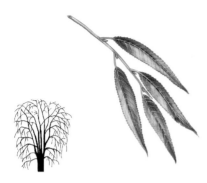

WEEPING WILLOW
Salix babylonica
Size: To 60 ft. (18 m)
Description: Easily distinguished by its short trunk and wide crown of drooping (weeping) branches. Narrow, finely-toothed leaves are evident from early spring until late autumn.
Habitat: Moist soils, along streams.
Comments: Native to China, this introduced willow is widely planted as an ornamental throughout Arizona.

WALNUTS

Deciduous trees noted for their aromatic leaves, drooping flower stalks called catkins and distinctive fruits with thick, grooved shells.

ARIZONA WALNUT
Juglans major
Size: 30-60 ft. (9-18 m)
Description: Tree with broad, spreading crown. Leaves are up to (12 in./30 cm) long and have 9-13 leaflets. Edible walnuts mature in early autumn.
Habitat: Moist soils in mountains, oak woodlands, desert grassland.
Comments: The nuts are a valuable food source for rodents and birds. The English walnut (*J. regia*) has been widely transplanted and is noted for its hard, durable wood.

ALDERS

Alders are fast-growing shrubs and trees with ragged crowns and deeply veined leaves. Their fruit is a distinctive woody cone.

ARIZONA ALDER
Alnus oblongifolia
Size: To 33 ft. (10 m)
Description: Small tree or large shrub with a rounded crown of spreading branches. Dark green leaves have toothed edges. Note cone-like fruit.
Habitat: Common near streams.
Comments: Grows at elevations between 4,000-7,000 ft. (1,200-2,100 m).

POPLARS

Found in moist habitats, these fast-growing trees are distinguished from willows by their drooping flower clusters (catkins). Alternate, unlobed leaves are toothed, generally heart-shaped and usually as long as they are wide. Green-white bark of young trees becomes grayish and furrowed as it matures.

FREMONT COTTONWOOD
Populus fremontii
Size: 50-80 ft. (15-24 m)
Description: Tree with a large, broad crown of spreading branches. Heart-shaped leaves have gently-toothed edges and flattened stems. Reddish flowers bloom in drooping catkins and are succeeded by capsules containing whitish cottony seeds.
Habitat: Wet soils near water.
Comments: In dry areas, cottonwoods indicate the presence of underground water.

QUAKING ASPEN
Populus tremuloides
Size: 40-60 ft. (12-18 m)
Description: Long, slender trunk supports a crown of spreading branches. Rounded, long-stemmed leaves rustle in the slightest breeze. Leaves turn yellow in autumn.
Habitat: Well-drained soils in a variety of locations.
Comments: Its twigs, leaves, catkins and bark are an important food source for wildlife.

LOMBARDY POPLAR
Populus nigra
Size: 30-60 ft. (9-18 m)
Description: Distinguished by its narrow crown of short, erect branches. Leaves are roughly triangular.
Habitat: Moist soils.
Comments: Introduced from Europe, it is now widely planted throughout Arizona as an ornamental.

OAKS

Oaks represent a group of important hardwoods. Generally, they are large trees with stout trunks and spreading crowns that produce acorns for fruit.

ARIZONA WHITE OAK
Quercus arizonica
Size: 16-65 ft. (4.8-20 m)
Description: Evergreen tree with a spreading crown of stout branches. Greenish leaves are about (2 in./5 cm) long and fuzzy beneath. Acorns are approximately (.5 in/1.3 cm) long.
Habitat: Rich soils in mountain valleys, foothills and woodlands in central and southeastern Arizona.
Comments: Common between elevations of 5,000-7,000 ft. (1,500-2,100 m).

EMORY OAK
Quercus emoryi
Size: 20-65 ft. (6-20 m)
Description: Evergreen shrub or tree with a short trunk and a spreading, rounded crown. Lance-shaped, leathery leaves (to 3 in./8 cm) have spiny margins. Cone-shaped acorns have a deep, scaly cup.
Habitat: Canyons, dry foothills, mountains and desert grasslands in central and southeastern Arizona.
Comments: Sweet acorns are consumed by squirrels, turkeys, quail and deer.

GAMBEL OAK
Quercus gambelii
Size: 15-65 ft. (4.5-20 m)
Description: Small to medium-sized tree or a thicket-forming shrub. Distinctive leaves have 5-9 deep lobes and are (3-6 in./8-15 cm) long. Acorns are broadly oval.
Habitat: Mountains and foothills.
Comments: Common in canyon country, it often grows in association with Arizona sycamore and Arizona cypress.

SYCAMORES

Large trees with very stout trunks and distinctive 'buttonball' fruits.

ARIZONA SYCAMORE
Platanus wrightii
Size: 30-100 ft. (9-30 m)
Description: Large trunk supports broad crown of spreading, whitish branches. The bark flakes off in irregular patches, making the trunk appear mottled. Star-shaped leaves have 3, 5 or 7 deep lobes. Fruiting balls grow in clusters of 3-7 per stalk.
Habitat: Moist soils along streams in valleys and canyons.
Comments: The largest and most abundant deciduous tree in the mountains of southeastern Arizona.

ROSES & ALLIES

A variable family of trees and shrubs found throughout North America.

CLIFFROSE
Cowania mexicana
Size: To 25 ft. (7.6 m)
Description: Shrub or small tree has small, dark-green leaves divided into 3-7 narrow lobes. Yellow to whitish flowers bloom May-August and are succeeded by unusual fruits with feathery tails.
Habitat: Dry soils, rocky slopes, often associated with junipers.
Comments: Hopi Indians used the wood for arrow shafts and the bark for clothing and rope.

BIRCHLEAF MOUNTAIN MAHOGANY
Cercocarpus betuloides
Size: To 25 ft. (7.6 m)
Description: Shrub or small tree with a spreading crown. Leaves are broadest above the middle. Yellowish flowers are succeeded by fruits with a feathery plume at the tip.
Habitat: Dry mountain slopes.
Comments: The term *cercocarpus* is derived from the Greek words for 'tail' and 'fruit.'

PEAS & ALLIES

Most members of this large family of trees, shrubs and herbs produce fruit in seed pods.

HONEY MESQUITE
Prosopis glandulosa
Size: To 20 ft. (6 m)
Description: Shrub or small tree with crown of crooked branches with sharp spines. Leaves are up to (10 in./25 cm) long and have 7-18 pairs of leaflets. Yellow flowers bloom in long spikes and are succeeded by narrow seed pods.
Habitat: Grasslands, sandy soils, deserts.
Comments: Wood is a source of firewood, charcoal and fence posts. Named for its sweet pods that Native Americans used in cakes and fermented drinks.

SCREWBEAN MESQUITE
Prosopis pubescens
Size: To 33 ft. (10 m)
Description: Small tree or shrub with twisted, spiny branches. Compound leaves have 5-8 pairs of leaflets that are covered with fine hairs. Distinctive pod is spiraled and (1-2 in./3-5 cm) long.
Habitat: Along streams in deserts.
Comments: Seeds and wood are used for same purposes as honey mesquite.

NEW MEXICO LOCUST
Robinia neomexicana
Size: To 25 ft. (7.6 m)
Description: Thicket-forming spiny tree or shrub. Long compound leaves (to 10 in./25 cm) have 13-21 leaflets that are finely haired. Showy pink-purple, pea-shaped flowers bloom in abundance in late spring. Seed pods are covered with bristly hairs.
Habitat: In woodlands and canyons.
Comments: Widely planted for erosion control, it is a valuable source of food for wildlife.

FOOTHILL PALO VERDE
Cercidium microphyllum
Size: To 20 ft. (6 m)
Description: Small tree or shrub with greenish bark that is leafless most of the year. Leaves have 4-10 pairs of tiny leaflets. Tree is blanketed with pale yellow blossoms in spring. Flowers are succeeded by seed pods.
Habitat: In deserts and on rocky hillsides, it often grows in association with saguaro cacti.
Comments: The similar blue palo verde (*C. floridum*) has blue-green bark, deeper yellow blossoms and is found primarily along floodplains and washes.

Arizona'a State Tree

IRONWOOD
Olneya tesota
Size: To 30 ft. (9 m)
Description: Gray-green, evergreen tree with spreading crown and a short, sometimes multi-branched, trunk. Leaves have a pair of short spines at their base and 2-10 pairs of leaflets. Seed pods are hairy and (2 in./5 cm) long.
Habitat: Rocky slopes and washes.
Comments: The extremely dense wood (one cubic foot weighs 66 lbs.) is valued for firewood and carving. Over harvesting is a problem since the tree grows very slowly.

CATCLAW
Acacia greggii
Size: To 23 ft. (7 m)
Description: Gray-green deciduous shrub has short, curved spines along its branches. Leaves have 2-3 side branches, each with 4-6 pairs of leaflets. Fuzzy yellow flowers bloom in elongated spikes between April-October, and are succeeded by reddish seed pods.
Habitat: Rocky slopes, desert flats.
Comments: A notorious local plant, its strong, curved spines readily tear clothing and flesh. Often forms impenetrable thickets.

OCOTILLOS

Distinctive family of desert shrubs and trees.

OCOTILLO
Fouquieria splendens
Size: To 30 ft. (9 m)
Description: Gray, thorny branches fan out from a central base. Small green leaves appear when there is adequate moisture, but drop off in times of drought. Bright red, tubular flowers bloom at stem tips in spring.
Habitat: Desert flats and rocky slopes.
Comments: Flowers are an important nectar source for migrating hummingbirds.

CALTROP FAMILY

Family of shrubs, herbs and trees found in hot climates.

CREOSOTE BUSH
Larrea tridentata
Size: To 10 ft. (3 m)
Description: One of the most common desert shrubs, it is told by its twisted, grayish stems and sparse foliage. Small yellow flowers (.5 in./1.3 cm) bloom throughout the year.
Habitat: Well-drained soils in deserts to elevations of 4,500 ft. (1,350 m).
Comments: Also called greasewood, it emits a pungent odor after it rains.

MAPLES

Maples are distinguished by their large, opposite-growing leaves and long-winged seed pairs. The leaves are especially conspicuous in autumn when they turn vivid shades of orange, red and yellow.

ROCKY MOUNTAIN MAPLE
Acer glabrum
Size: To 30 ft. (9 m)
Description: Shrub or small tree. Leaves are up to (5 in./13 cm) long and have reddish stalks. Greenish flowers bloom in drooping clusters in spring, and are succeeded by winged seed pairs in late summer.
Habitat: Moist soils.
Comments: Found at mountain elevations above 5,000 ft. (1,500 m).

BIGNONIA FAMILY

Family of mainly tropical shrubs, trees, vines and herbs.

DESERT WILLOW
Chilopsis linearis
Size: To 30 ft. (9 m)
Description: Shrub or small tree with narrow, willow-like leaves. Showy whitish, tubular flowers bloom in May-June and are succeeded by long seed pods.
Habitat: Along arroyos (dry washes) in deserts and grasslands.
Comments: Has spreading roots and is often planted for erosion control.

COMPOSITES

The largest family of plants in North America, it includes sunflowers, asters, daisies, lettuce and zinnias to name a few. There are over 19,000 species worldwide.

RABBITBRUSH
Ericameria nauseosus
Size: 3-7 ft. (.9-2.1 m)
Description: Small shrub with wiry, erect, hairy stems. Terminal clusters of small yellow flowers bloom August-October.
Habitat: Dry plains, along slopes, washes.
Comments: An important food source for jackrabbits and deer. Often grows in association with sagebrush.

BRITTLEBRUSH
Encelia farinosa
Size: To 5 ft. (1.5 m)
Description: Rounded evergreen shrub has leaves covered with white hairs. Bright, daisy-like yellow flowers bloom above the foliage between March-May.
Habitat: Dry slopes, gravelly plains, desert washes.
Comments: The plant may bloom at other times of the year following heavy rains. Fragrant stems were once burned as incense.

BOX FAMILY

Only a single member of this Family is found in Arizona.

JOJOBA
Simmondsia chinensis
Size: To 7 ft. (2.1 m)
Description: Gray-green shrub
has thick, short-stemmed leaves to
(1.5 in./4 cm) long. Fruits are nut-like.
Habitat: Dry, rocky slopes, by washes.
Comments: Pioneers and Native
Americans roasted the nuts and ground
them for use as a coffee substitute.

PALMS, YUCCAS & CACTI

These common desert plants are familiar sights since most have been
widely transplanted in urban areas. All are evergreen and differ from other
trees by having trunks that lack growth rings.

CALIFORNIA FAN PALM
Washingtonia filifera
Size: 20-50 ft. (6-15 m)
Description: Told at a glance by its
crown of large, fan-shaped leaves
and the shaggy sack of dead leaves
hanging beneath it.
Habitat: Moist soils in southwestern
Arizona.
Comments: The only palm native
to the Southwest, it has been widely
cultivated in urban areas. The state's
most noted grove grows in Palm Canyon
in the Kofa National Wildlife Refuge.

CANARY PALM
Phoenix canariensis
Size: To 50 ft. (15 m)
Description: Tree with stout, straight
trunk and enormous, feathery, evergreen
leaves (12-20 ft./3.6-6 m) long.
Habitat: Moist soils.
Comments: Introduced more than a
century ago, it is commonly planted
along streets.

DATE PALM
Phoenix dactylifera
Size: To 75 ft. (23 m)
Description: Distinguished by its stout trunk and crown of ascending palm leaves. Trunk is roughened by the vestiges of dead leaves. Large clusters of small yellow flowers are succeeded by clusters of pulpy fruits.
Habitat: Moist soils.
Comments: A non-native ornamental.

CENTURY PLANT
Agave parryi
Size: To 8 ft. (2.4 m)
Description: Tall, candelabra-like flowering stalk rises from a rosette of gray-green leaves. Yellow flowers bloom in dense clusters during summer months.
Habitat: Rocky slopes in central Arizona.
Comments: Plant takes several years to flower and blooms only once. A number of similar species of agave are found in Arizona including *A. chrysantha* and *A. deserti*. All were a source of food, medicine, tools and fiber for Native Americans.

JOSHUA-TREE
Yucca brevifolia
Size: 15-30 ft. (4.5-9 m)
Description: A many-branched tree with terminal tufts of short, stiff, dagger-like leaves to (8 in./20 cm) long. Clusters of yellow tubular flowers bloom March-May and are succeeded by oblong fruits (2-4 in./5-10 cm) long.
Habitat: Dry soil on deserts, plains, hillsides in western Arizona.
Comments: Tree is home to as many as 25 species of birds. Fruit is a valuable source of food for desert wildlife.

MOHAVE YUCCA
Yucca schidigera
Size: 10-16 ft. (3-4.8 m)
Description: Tree or shrub with upright branches and prominent, dagger-like leaves. White flowers bloom in spring and are succeeded by cylindrical fruits.
Habitat: Dry soils in the Mohave Desert in northwest Arizona.
Comments: Indians obtained food, blankets and ropes from this plant. All yuccas are members of the lily family of flowering plants.

SOAPTREE YUCCA
Yucca elata
Size: 10-17 ft. (3-5.1 m)
Description: Tree or small shrub with one or more trunks. Leaves are grass-like, sharp-pointed and about (2 ft./60 cm) long. Old leaves form a thatch on the trunk. A slender flowering stalk emerges in spring and supports a dense cluster of bell-shaped white flowers.
Habitat: Deserts and desert grasslands in central and southern Arizona.
Comments: A soap substitute is made from its roots and trunk.

Arizona's State Flower

SAGUARO
Carnegiea gigantea
Size: 20-50 ft. (6-15 m)
Description: Upright, stout trunk is ribbed vertically. Trunk usually grows 'arms' when 50-100 years old. Waxy white flowers bloom in May and are succeeded by fleshy red fruits in June.
Habitat: Rocky desert soils in southern Arizona.
Comments: The symbol of southwestern deserts, the saguaro is an important food source and nesting site for desert animals including woodpeckers, martins, owls, lizards and woodrats, to name a few. The fruits are used to make jellies and wine.

ORGAN PIPE CACTUS
Stenocereus thurberi
Size: 10-20 ft. (3-6 m)
Description: Many upright, ribbed stems branch from a common base. Pinkish, night-blooming flowers occur April-August.
Habitat: Rocky soils.
Comments: Native to the area protected by the Organ Pipe Cactus National Monument in southern Arizona.

TEDDYBEAR CHOLLA
Opuntia bigelovii
Size: 3-9 ft. (.9-2.7 m)
Description: A small, fuzzy-looking cactus with branches covered with numerous inch-long, barbed spines. Greenish-yellow flowers bloom at branch tips in summer and are succeeded by green, fleshy fruits.
Habitat: Dry, open areas in deserts.
Comments: Beware of this cute-sounding plant: the sharp-spined sections detach at the slightest touch and are extremely painful to remove. One of several species of cholla that include shrubby and tree-like cacti with jointed branches.

JUMPING CHOLLA
Opuntia fulgida
Size: To 15 ft. (4.5 m)
Description: Very spiny tree or shrub with a short trunk and numerous stout, jointed branches. Pinkish flowers bloom in spring and summer months and are succeeded by greenish, pear-shaped fruits.
Habitat: Desert plains and gentle slopes between 1,000-4,000 ft. (304-1,219 m).
Comments: Also called the chainfruit cholla, its fruits grow in hanging clusters and may remain attached for several years.

BEAVERTAIL CACTUS
Opuntia basilaris
Size: Pads to 18 in. (45 cm)
Description: Jointed, flattened cactus segments grow in clumps. Showy pink flowers bloom February-June.
Habitat: Rocky slopes in deserts.
Comments: Widely planted as an ornamental in southern Arizona. Clumps may grow up to 6 ft. (1.8 m) in diameter.

HEDGEHOG CACTUS
Echinocereus triglochidiatus
Size: To 18 in. (45 cm)
Description: Ribbed cylindrical stems grow in clusters. Beautiful, scarlet-orange flowers bloom April-May.
Habitat: Deserts, oak woodlands.
Comments: There are a number of similar species found in Arizona.

DESERT PRICKLY PEAR CACTUS
Opuntia phaeacantha
Size: To 3 ft. (90 cm)
Description: A sprawling or erect cactus with jointed, prickly pads. Red-centered, yellow flowers bloom April-June.
Habitat: Deserts throughout Arizona.
Comments: There are more than 20 species of prickly pear cactus in the U.S. Both the fruit 'tuna' and the pads are consumed by humans and wildlife.

FISHHOOK CACTUS
Mammillaria microcarpa
Size: To 6 in. (15 cm)
Description: Plant grows singly or in clumps. Key field mark is long, hooked spines.
Habitat: Rocky areas.
Comments: The term 'mammillaria' refers to the nipple-like projections on the stem.

BARREL CACTUS
Ferocactus acanthodes
Size: 3-10 ft. (.9-3 m)
Description: Cylindrical cactus has 20 to 28 ribs. Yellow to orange flowers bloom in spring.
Habitat: Dry hills, gravelly slopes.
Comments: Its succulent stem is able to absorb large amounts of water during short rainy spells. In emergency situations, the inner pulp can be mashed and sucked to obtain water.

BEEHIVE CACTUS
Coryphantha vivipara
Size: To 6 in. (15 cm)
Description: Ball-shaped cactus grows singly or in clumps. Stem is densely covered in spines. Pinkish flowers bloom May-July.
Habitat: Rocky and sandy areas in woodlands.
Comments: Often grows in association with creosote bush or in pinyon-juniper woods.

BUCKHORN CHOLLA
Opuntia acanthocarpa
Size: To 6 ft. (1.8 m)
Description: Cylindrical 'joints' are up to 20 in. (50 cm) long and are covered with knob-like projections. Spines occur in clusters of 12 or more.
Habitat: Sandy areas.
Comments: Also called deer-horn cactus, it is an open, branching cactus that may be shrub- or tree-like.

BANANA YUCCA
Yucca baccata
Size: To 5 ft. (1.5 m)
Description: Long spikey leaves grow in basal rosette. Flower stalk is densely covered with waxy, bell-shaped flowers. Stalk is usually slightly taller than leaves.
Habitat: Open rocky slopes.
Comments: Occurs between elevations of 3,000-8,000 ft. (914-2,438 m).

WHAT ARE WILDFLOWERS?

Wildflowers are soft-stemmed flowering plants, smaller than trees or shrubs, that grow anew each year. Some regenerate annually from the same root-stock (perennials), while others grow from seeds and last a single season (annuals). Most have flowering stems bearing colorful blossoms that ripen into fruits as the growing season progresses. The flowering stem typically grows upright, but may be climbing, creeping or trailing. Wildflowers range from weeds and reeds to roses and buttercups, and are found almost every-where in Arizona.

The species in this section have been grouped according to color rather than Family in order to facilitate field identification. The color groups used are:

- White
- Yellow, Orange and Green
- Red and Pink
- Blue and Purple

HOW TO IDENTIFY WILDFLOWERS

After noting color, examine the shape of the flower heads. Are they daisy-like, bell-shaped or odd in appearance? How are they arranged on the plant? Do they occur singly or in clusters? Are the flower heads upright or drooping? Pay close attention to the leaves and how they are arranged on the stem. Refer to the illustrations and text to confirm its size, habitat and blooming period.

N.B. – *The blooming periods of flowers can vary depending on latitude, elevation and the weather. The dates given are meant to serve as general guidelines only.*

Remember that flowers are wildlife and should be treated as such. Many species have been seriously depleted due to loss of habitat and overpicking. In many areas, once-abundant species are now rare. Bring along a sketch-book and camera to record the flowers you see instead of picking them. This will help ensure there are more blossoms for you and others to enjoy in years to come.

N.B. – *It is illegal to collect most of Arizona's native plants. Check with the Department of Forestry regarding protected and endangered species.*

FLOWER STRUCTURE

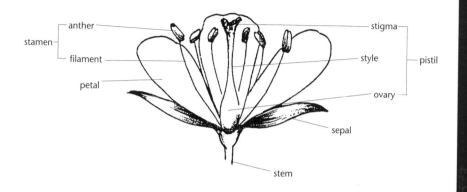

stamen
- anther
- filament

petal

stigma
style
ovary

pistil

sepal

stem

FLOWER SHAPES

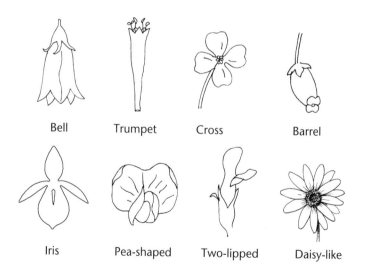

Bell

Trumpet

Cross

Barrel

Iris

Pea-shaped

Two-lipped

Daisy-like

WHITE FLOWERS

SACRED DATURA
Datura meteloides
Size: To 5 ft. (1.5 m)
Description: Large, white trumpet-shaped flowers arise from coarse, rank-smelling, gray-green foliage. Fragrant flowers bloom May-October, and are succeeded by round, prickly fruits.
Habitat: Sandy soil, gullies, woodlands.
Comments: Flowers bloom in evenings and are pollinated at night by sphinx moths. All parts of the plant are poisonous.

DESERT AJO LILY
Hesperocallis undulata
Size: To 5 ft. (1.5 m)
Description: Large, funnel-shaped white flowers are unmistakable. Narrow leaves have wavy edges. Blooms March-May.
Habitat: Sandy soils in southwestern Arizona.
Comments: Easily spotted when driving through the low desert region. Plant has edible, garlicky bulbs and is also called the ajo lily (ajo = garlic).

BLADDER CAMPION
Silene cucubalis
Size: To 3 ft. (90 cm)
Description: Upright, smooth-leaved plant with forked clusters of swollen white flowers. Blooms in summer.
Habitat: Disturbed areas, roadsides.
Comments: A beautiful weed found throughout the U.S.

PRICKLY POPPY
Argemone pleiacantha
Size: To 4 ft. (1.2 m)
Description: Distinctive yellow-centered, white flower with tissue-thin petals. Stems, leaves and seed pods are covered in prickles. Blooms March-October.
Habitat: Sandy soil, dry hillsides, woodlands, roadsides.
Comments: All parts of the plant are poisonous. Several similar species exist that have yellow-to-pinkish flowers.

COW PARSNIP
Heracleum lanatum
Size: To 10 ft. (3 m)
Description: A large, conspicuous plant with deeply lobed leaves growing along the length of its thick, hollow stem. Dense, flattened clusters of creamy white flowers bloom July-August.
Habitat: Common in moist fields and woods.
Comments: Though non-poisonous, it resembles similar plants, like the water hemlock, which are deadly.

WHITE CLOVER
Trifolium repens
Size: 4-24 in. (10-60 cm)
Description: Long-stemmed, dark green leaves have three oval leaflets and grow densely along creeping, mat-forming stems. Rounded white flowers bloom April-September.
Habitat: Common in fields, lawns and disturbed areas.
Comments: It is an excellent nectar producer and a favorite of bees.

FRAGRANT WATERLILY
Nymphaea odorata
Size: To 6 in. (15 cm)
Description: Common aquatic plant is distinguished by its large, many-rayed, white to pinkish, yellow-centered flowers. Round leafpads are notched at their base. Blooms nearly year-round.
Habitat: Ponds, lakes, streams.
Comments: This floating plant is rooted to the bottom and usually grows in water less than 8 ft. (2.4 m) deep.

ARROWHEAD
Sagittaria latifolia
Size: To 3 ft. (90 cm)
Description: Small, white lily-like flowers bloom above arrow-shaped leaves May-August.
Habitat: Ponds, slow streams, marshes, ditches.
Comments: The plant produces underground tubers that were an important food source for early settlers.

YARROW
Achillea millefolium
Size: To 40 in. (1 m)
Description: A long, unbranched stem supports dense clusters of round, yellow-centered daisy-like flowers. Each flower has 4 to 6 white (occasionally pinkish) rays. The unusual fern-like leaves are a good field mark. Blooms June-September.
Habitat: Common in ditches, fields and disturbed areas near woodlands.
Comments: An aromatic herb, it is also known as milfoil.

BINDWEED
Convolvulus arvensis
Size: To 3 ft. (90 cm)
Description: A twining plant with beautiful, white-to-pinkish funnel-shaped flowers. Blooms May-October.
Habitat: Gardens, disturbed areas, fields, farmlands.
Comments: Regarded as a weed by many, it is very difficult to eradicate because of its deep roots. It is a member of the morning-glory family.

COMMON ICE PLANT
Mesembryanthemum crystallinum
Size: Stems 8-24 in. (20-60 cm)
Description: A creeping plant with beaded, glistening stems. Showy white or pinkish flowers bloom April-October.
Habitat: Sandy soils in southwestern Arizona.
Comments: The flowers open fully only in direct sunlight.

ENGLISH DAISY
Bellis perennis
Size: To 10 in. (25 cm)
Description: Slender, leafless stalk supports a single, yellow-centered white flower with numerous rays. Basal leaves are rounded. Blooms March-September.
Habitat: Fields, disturbed areas, roadsides.
Comments: A common lawn weed introduced from Europe.

PHLOX
Phlox spp.
Size: To 20 in. (50 cm)
Description: Sprawling herbs or small shrub with numerous showy, five-lobed, yellow-centered flowers. Flowers range in color from pink and lavender to yellow and white blooms April-September.
Habitat: Dry soils in a variety of habitats.
Comments: A species common to central Arizona is the white-flowered desert phlox (*P. tenuifolia*).

QUEEN ANNE'S LACE
Daucus carota
Size: To 4 ft. (1.2 m)
Description: Distinguished by large, flat-topped flowers clusters and lacy foliage. The flower clusters become cup-shaped as they age.
Habitat: Roadsides, waste areas.
Comments: Introduced species is a relative of the garden carrot. The plant closely resembles the toxic poison hemlock.

DESERT STAR
Monoptilon belloides
Size: To 3 in. (8 cm)
Description: Low-growing plant has a yellow central disk surrounded by white rays that are often tinged in pink or lavender.
Habitat: Sandy and rocky soils in western Arizona.
Comments: Will bloom in profusion following rainstorms but is often obscured by other wildflowers because of its low height.

DUNE PRIMROSE
Oenothera deltoides
Size: To 12 in. (30 cm)
Description: Grayish plant has delicate flowers with tissue like petals. Leaves are diamond-shaped.
Habitat: Deserts.
Comments: Flowers bloom in the early evening and close in early morning. When a plant dies, its stems curve upward forming a basket-like shape. Also known as birdcage primrose.

YELLOW, ORANGE & GREEN FLOWERS

GOLDEN COLUMBINE
Aquilegia chrysantha
Size: To 4 ft. (1.2 m)
Description: Bushy plant with upward-pointing yellow flowers with prominent spurs. Stamens project well beyond flower margin. Blooms July-August.
Habitat: Moist woodlands.
Comments: The similar longspur columbine (*A. longissima*) found in southern Arizona has spurs more than twice as long (to 8 in./20 cm).

ARIZONA MULE'S EAR
Wyethia arizonica
Size: To 10 in. (25 cm)
Description: Yellow sunflower-like flowers strikingly contrast a background of clustered, large leaves that resemble a mule's ears. Blooms June-August.
Habitat: Hillsides, meadows in foothills and mountains.
Comments: The similar sandpaper mule's ear (*W. scabra*), found in northern Arizona, has narrower leaves with a sandpaper-like surface.

PRINCE'S PLUME
Stanleya pinnata
Size: To 5 ft. (1.5 m)
Description: Smooth, erect stems support slender, feathery spike of yellow flowers. Blooms April-September.
Habitat: Deserts and mountain foothills.
Comments: The flower spikes are often conspicuous in the desert. Also called the Paiute cabbage, its leaves were once used for potherbs.

ARIZONA POPPY
Kallstroemia grandiflora
Size: Stems to 3 ft. (90 cm) long.
Description: Creeping plant with bright-orange, bowl-shaped flowers with a crimson center. Blooms July-October.
Habitat: Deserts.
Comments: Poppy-like flower that often blankets entire hillsides during mid-summer in southern Arizona.

SNAKEWEED
Gutierrezia sarothrae
Size: To 3 ft. (90 cm)
Description: Small, rounded green shrub is smothered with small yellow flowers during summer and autumn months.
Habitat: Deserts, dry wooded slopes. Often associated with junipers.
Comments: Also called broomweed, pioneers used to bundle stems to make brooms.

CHINCHWEED
Pectis papposa
Size: To 8 in. (20 cm)
Description: Low, leafy plant supports small clusters of yellow flowers at its stem tips. Lobed leaves have spines near their base. Blooms July-October.
Habitat: Sandy soils in deserts and open areas at low-to-middle elevations.
Comments: Often grows in profusion along roadsides.

CREAMCUPS
Platystemon californicus
Size: To 12 in. (30 cm)
Description: Hairy plant with narrow, opposite leaves. Bowl-shaped, six-petaled yellow flowers bloom atop slender stalks March-May.
Habitat: Moist meadows, fields, hillsides.
Comments: Grows in dense colonies and often covers entire fields.

GOLDFIELDS
Lasthenia chrysostoma
Size: To 10 in. (25 cm)
Description: Slender, reddish stems with opposite, narrow leaves support small yellow flowers. Blooms March-May.
Habitat: Poor soils, open, dry areas.
Comments: When enough moisture is available, this flower literally blankets open areas with gold.

TREE TOBACCO
Nicotiana glauca
Size: To 26 ft. (8 m)
Description: Shrub or small tree with open, spreading branches. Tubular flowers bloom at night in spreading clusters between April-November.
Habitat: Roadsides, disturbed areas, washes in southern Arizona.
Comments: Common along roadsides, it is one of 12 species of plants containing nicotine found in North America.

MEXICAN GOLDPOPPY
Eschscholzia mexicana
Size: To 16 in. (40 cm)
Description: Distinguished by its delicate yellow-orange flowers and blue-green, fern-like leaves. Flowers range in color from white to orange and bloom March-May.
Habitat: Open areas, dry slopes.
Comments: The flowers are light-sensitive and close at night. Plants often blanket huge areas.

COMMON PLANTAIN
Plantago major
Size: To 20 in. (50 cm)
Description: Large, tough basal leaves are finely toothed with deep longitudinal veins. Tiny greenish flowers bloom in a slender spike.
Habitat: Very common in lawns, gardens and disturbed areas.
Comments: An introduced weed widespread throughout the country.

BUFFALO GOURD
Cucurbita foetidissima
Size: To 15 in. (38 cm)
Description: Large, triangular leaves grow along prostrate stems. Yellow, funnel-shaped flowers bloom May-August, often hiding beneath the leaves. The fruit, a round, striped gourd, is very visible in winter.
Habitat: Open areas.
Comments: The gourds are eaten by desert animals and are often dried and painted by artisans.

DESERT MARIGOLD
Baileya multiradiata
Size: To 20 in. (50 cm)
Description: Bright yellow, daisy-like flowers bloom atop slender stems rising from a grayish, leafy base. Blooms May-November.
Habitat: Rocky and sandy soils.
Comments: Very common along roadsides. A short-lived plant, it reseeds readily and is visible nearly year-round.

COMMON SUNFLOWER
Helianthus annuus
Size: To 13 ft. (3.9 m)
Description: Tall, leafy plant with a branching stem supporting numerous yellow, dark-centered flowers. Blooms June-September.
Habitat: Roadsides, disturbed areas, open fields.
Comments: Flowers follow the sun across the sky each day.

YELLOW SALSIFY
Tragopogon dubius
Size: 15-30 in. (38-75 cm)
Description: Brnaching hollow stems have grass-like leaves. Pale yellow flowerhead is distinctive.
Habitat: Roadsides, waste areas.
Comments: The flowers are succeeded seed-like fruits covered in feathery brown bristles.

GOLDENROD
Solidago canadensis
Size: To 5 ft. (1.5 m)
Description: Tall, leafy plant with spreading, arched clusters of tiny yellow flowers. Leaves are hairy with three distinct veins. Blooms May-September.
Habitat: Meadows, pastures, open forests.
Comments: Widespread to the point that it is considered a nuisance in some areas.

SUBALPINE BUTTERCUP
Ranunculus eschscholtzii
Size: To 10 in. (25 cm)
Description: Shiny, yellow flower with five overlapping petals and smooth, oval leaves. Blooms June-August.
Habitat: Mountain meadows, rocky slopes, fields.
Comments: One of over several similar species of buttercup found in Arizona.

DEVIL'S CLAW
Proboscidea althaeifolia
Size: To 12 in. (30 cm)
Description: Creeping plant with trailing stems covered with shiny, scalloped leaves. Yellowish flowers bloom June-September and are succeeded by distinctive curved seed pods (to 5 in./13 cm long).
Habitat: Sandy soil in deserts and open areas.
Comments: As the greenish fruits mature, they blacken and the tips split into two hooked 'devil's claws'.

COMMON DANDELION
Taraxacum officinale
Size: To 12 in. (30 cm)
Description: Told by its elongate, toothed leaves and shaggy yellow flowers that bloom frequently throughout the growing season.
Habitat: Open and grassy areas.
Comments: Its leaves can be used in salads and its blossoms for wine-making.

HOOKER'S EVENING PRIMROSE
Oenothera hookeri
Size: To 3 ft. (90 cm)
Description: Tall plant with long, slender leaves. Large, four-petaled yellow flowers bloom June-September.
Habitat: Roadsides and grassy slopes from low-to-middle elevations.
Comments: As the common name suggests, the flowers open near the end of the day.

COMMON MONKEY FLOWER
Mimulus guttatus
Size: To 5 ft. (1.5 m)
Description: Trumpet-shaped yellow flowers have dark-spotted, hairy throats. Oval leaves are coarsely toothed; lower leaves are stalked, upper ones are clasping. Flowers bloom in loose terminal clusters March-September.
Habitat: Wet areas, meadows, and ditches at most elevations.
Comments: Red monkey flowers (*M. lewisii*) are also found in Arizona.

ST.JOHN'S WORT
Hypericum perforatum
Size: To 3 ft. (90 cm)
Description: Branching, leafy stem supports a cluster of star-shaped yellow flowers, often with black dots near the tips. Blooms June-September.
Habitat: Pastures, roadsides and waste areas.
Comments: A plant extraction is a common herbal remedy.

BUTTERFLYWEED
Asclepias tuberosa
Size: To 3 ft. (90 cm)
Description: Bright orange, star-like flowers bloom in large clusters May-September. Stem may be erect or crawling. Alternate leaves are lance-shaped.
Habitat: Meadows, fields, roadsides, prairies.
Comments: Unlike other milkweed species, it lacks milky sap.

WOOLLY MULLEIN
Verbascum thapsus
Size: To 7 ft. (2.1 m)
Description: Tall leafy plant that tapers from a broad base to a slender spike of yellow flowers. Flowers bloom a few at a time throughout summer.
Habitat: Fields and waste areas.
Comments: Miners used to make torches from these plants by dipping them in tallow.

RED & PINK FLOWERS

FIREWEED
Chamerion angustifolium
Size: To 7 ft. (2.1 m)
Description: Distinguished by a long conical spike of bright pink, 4-petaled flowers. Blooms June-September.
Habitat: Very common in open woodlands, clearings and burned-out areas at upper elevations.
Comments: Often grows in dense colonies and tints entire fields a shade of pink.

DESERT MARIPOSA LILY
Calochortus kennedyi
Size: To 8 in. (20 cm)
Description: Short stems support small cluster of up to 6 tulip-like, orange-to-yellow flowers. Blooms March-June. Leaves are narrow and grass-like.
Habitat: Dry soil in deserts and pinyon-juniper woodlands in central and southern Arizona.
Comments: One of several species of marioposa lilies found in the southwest.

SKYROCKET
Ipomopsis aggregata
Size: To 7 ft. (2.1 m)
Description: Slender stems support clusters of bright red, tubular flowers resembling exploded fireworks. Blooms May-September.
Habitat: Open woodlands, ponderosa pine forest, dry hillsides.
Comments: Also called skunk flower, for its rank-smelling leaves.

OWL CLOVER
Orthocarpus purpurea
Size: To 15 in. (38 cm)
Description: Small plant has showy brush-like spike of showy red-to purple-tipped floral bracts. Small pouch-shaped white-to-yellow flowers are found within the bracts. Blooms March-May.
Habitat: Open areas.
Comments: Flowers are thought by some to resemble roosting owls that peer from beneath the bracts.

DESERT FOUR O'CLOCK
Mirabilis multiflora
Size: To 18 in. (45 cm)
Description: Showy pink, tubular flowers open in the evenings – often around 4 o'clock. Heart-shaped, opposite leaves grow along the stem length. Blooms April-September.
Habitat: Deserts, grasslands.
Comments: There are more than 100 species of four o'clock found in America's deserts. Related species include verbenas and bougainvilleas.

CANADA THISTLE
Cirsium arvense
Size: To 5 ft. (1.5 m)
Description: Tall plant with scalloped, prickly leaves and puffy pink flowers. Blooms May-October.
Habitat: Fields, ditches, waste areas.
Comments: This ubiquitous weed is common throughout North America, Asia and Europe. Flowers are sweet-smelling and rich in nectar.

BEARDTONGUE
Penstemon barbatus
Size: To 5 ft. (1.5 m)
Description: Slender, wispy plant with drooping, tubular blossoms. A 'beard' of yellowish hairs typically dangles from the flower's lower lip. Blooms May-September.
Habitat: Open woodlands, rocky hillsides at upper elevations.
Comments: Plant's sweet nectar attracts myriad hummingbirds and insects.

COMMON FLEABANE
Erigeron philadelphicus
Size: To 3 ft. (90 cm)
Description: Narrow leaves clasp the stem and are densely clustered at the plant base. Pink to white ray flowers bloom in loose clusters June-August.
Habitat: Moist meadows, open woods.
Comments: One of several fleabanes found in Arizona. The plants were once hung in houses to keep fleas away. Similar to asters, the flower rays are narrower and more numerous.

CARDINAL FLOWER
Lobelia cardinalis
Size: To 4 ft. (1.2 m)
Description: Plant with spike of striking, red tubular flowers. Red stamen tubes project beyond the flower margins. Blooms June-October.
Habitat: Wet, open areas, moist woods.
Comments: Also called scarlet lobelia, its flowers are an important nectar source for hummingbirds.

DESERT PRIMROSE
Primula parryi
Size: To 15 in. (38 cm)
Description: Stout, leafless stalk supports a cluster of 3-12 bright pink, yellow-centered flowers. Basal leaves are oblong. Blooms June-August.
Habitat: Shaded woodlands, along waterways.
Comments: Common along trails in the foothills and mountains in northern Arizona.

STORKSBILL
Erodium cicutarium
Size: To 12 in. (30 cm)
Description: Crawling, red-stemmed plant gives rise to clusters of small, pinkish flowers (.4 in./1 cm). Named for distinctive 'beaked' seed pods that point upwards.
Habitat: Deserts, open and disturbed areas.
Comments: A harbinger of spring each year, it blooms between February and June.

WILD ROSE
Rosa **spp.**
Size: To 5 ft. (1.5 m)
Description: A prickly shrub with broad, pink, five-petalled, sweet-smelling flowers. Blooms April-September.
Habitat: Open areas and woodlands at middle to upper elevations.
Comments: Flowers are succeeded by fruits called hips that are rich in vitamin C and often used in teas.

INDIAN PAINTBRUSH
Castilleja **spp.**
Size: To 3 ft. (90 cm)
Description: Ragged red wildflower often grows in dense colonies. Blooms March-October.
Habitat: Woodlands and mountain meadows.
Comments: Related to snapdragons, paintbrushes occur in a variety of colors. Many are often parasitic on the roots of other plants.

FAIRY SLIPPER
Calypso bulbosa
Size: To 8 in. (20 cm)
Description: Stunning flower bloom atop a slender stalk. Single basal leaf is pleated.
Habitat: Moist woods in NE Arizona
Comments: One of the most widespread native orchids in North America.

SHOOTING STAR
Dodecatheon pulchellum
Size: To 20 in. (50 cm)
Description: Graceful plant with drooping, dart-like reddish flowers with inverted petals exposing yellow stamen tube. Blooms May-August.
Habitat: Moist soils in meadows, fields and open woodlands in east-central Arizona.
Comments: Several similar species are found in Arizona. Related to primroses and cyclamens.

PIPSISSEWA
Chimaphila umbellata
Size: To 10 in. (25 cm)
Description: Leathery, evergreen leaves are coarsely-toothed and whorled around the stem. Small, saucer-shaped, waxy pink flowers. Bloom in nodding clusters of 3-10 between June-August.
Habitat: Found in cool, moist coniferous forests.
Comments: Leaves were once used as a tea substitute by early settlers.

PINE DROPS
Pterospora andromedea
Size: To 3 ft. (90 cm)
Description: Slender, hairy, red-brown stalks covered with small, red-to-white, egg-shaped flowers.
Habitat: Coniferous forests.
Comments: Is a root parasite of conifers that also feeds on decaying matter in cool forests. Commonly associated with ponderosa pine.

DESERT GLOBEMALLOW
Sphaeralcea ambigua
Size: To 40 in. (1 m)
Description: Hairy, branching plant with striking red-orange flowers. Leaves are three-lobed and coarsely toothed. Blooms March-June.
Habitat: Deserts.
Comments: Genus name refers to the spherical fruit that succeeds the flowers.

FIREWHEEL
Gaillardia pulchella
Size: To 2 ft. (60 cm)
Description: Fiery pinwheel-shaped flowers have red rays tipped in yellow. Inner disk is maroon and dome-shaped. Blooms May-September.
Habitat: Sandy soils, disturbed areas, roadsides.
Comments: Conspicuous along roadsides, they often blanket open areas covering several acres.

BLUE & PURPLE FLOWERS

ARIZONA LUPINE
Lupinus arizonicus
Size: To 2 ft. (60 cm)
Description: Purplish, pea-shaped flowers are highlighted against bright green, star-shaped leaves. Blooms January-May.
Habitat: Low deserts.
Comments: Very common in the western half of Arizona. The similar Palmer lupine (*L. palmeri*) is the most common lupine in ponderosa pine forests.

MONKSHOOD
Aconitum columbianum
Size: To 6 ft. (1.8 m)
Description: A leafy plant with deep blue flowers resembling a monk's habit. Blooms June-September.
Habitat: Mountain meadows, moist woods.
Comments: Related species provide medicine, and many are poisonous.

SHOWY MILKWEED
Asclepias speciosa
Size: To 4 ft. (1.2 m)
Description: Red-purplish, horned flowers bloom in tight clusters May-August. Large, fleshy leaves are finely haired. In autumn, long seed pods split open to release thousands of conspicuous, long-plumed seeds.
Habitat: Dry soils in disturbed areas and ditches, open forests.
Comments: Both the leaves and stems secrete a sticky fluid to protect the flowers from crawling insects.

DESERT SAND VERBENA
Abronia villosa
Size: To 10 in. (25 cm)
Description: Small, sticky creeping plants with dense clusters of tiny lavender flowers. Opposite leaves have wavy edges. Blooms February-October.
Habitat: Deserts in sandy soil.
Comments: Plants often form a carpet covering miles of open desert following rains.

CHICORY
Cichorium intybus
Size: To 6 ft. (1.8 m)
Description: Wheel-shaped, pale-blue flowers bloom atop slender branching stems April-October.
Habitat: Fields, roadsides, disturbed areas.
Comments: The roots can be roasted to make a coffee substitute. An introduced species.

AWL-LEAF ASTER
Aster subaltus
Size: To 3 ft. (90 cm)
Description: Distinguished by its purplish-to-pinkish, yellow-centered flowers with broad rays. Narrow leaves are awl-shaped and clasp the stem its entire length. Blooms July-October.
Habitat: Wet soils in meadows and forests.
Comments: One of several species of aster found in Arizona. All have the familiar starburst flower heads.

BLUE DICKS
Dichelostemma pulchellum
Size: To 20 in. (50 cm)
Description: Long, slender flower stalk supports a cluster of blue-to-pink flower tubes that resemble inflated balls. Blooms April-June.
Habitat: Open grassy areas.
Comments: Common at lower elevations.

DAYFLOWER
Commelina communis
Size: To 3 ft. (90 cm)
Description: Sprawling plant has upright stems supporting striking flowers with two large, rounded blue upper petals and a small white lower petal. Blooms May-October.
Habitat: Open woodlands, weedy areas in SE Arizona.
Comments: Named for its short-lived blossoms. Introduced from Asia.

HAREBELL
Campanula rotundifolia
Size: To 20 in. (50 cm)
Description: Plant with grass-like leaves and a drooping cluster of pale blue, bell-shaped flowers. Blooms June-September.
Habitat: Dry mountain meadows, rocky slopes.
Comments: Also called Scotch bluebells.

OYSTERPLANT
Tragopogon porrifolius
Size: To 4 ft. (1.2 m)
Description: Purple flower head blooms atop a swollen stem during summer.
Habitat: Fields, waste areas.
Comments: Also called oyster plant, its root has the flavor of oysters when cooked.

AMERICAN VETCH
Vicia americana
Size: To 4 ft. (1.2 m) long
Description: A climbing vine with clusters of 4-10 purplish, pea-shaped flowers. Flowers turn blue as they age. Blooms April-July.
Habitat: Open mountain woodlands, roadsides.
Comments: Similar to a number of wild pea plants.

ROCKY MOUNTAIN IRIS
Iris missouriensis
Size: To 20 in. (50 cm)
Description: Slender stalks support large blue to violet flowers. Petals have a central yellow-orange stripe and purple veins are often visible. Narrow basal leaves are sword-shaped. Blooms May-July.
Habitat: Wet mountain habitats.
Comments: Often grow in dense clumps in meadows and along streams. Leaf fibers were once used to make rope.

BLUE-EYED GRASS
Sisyrinchium angustifolium
Size: To 2 ft. (60 cm)
Description: Slender stems support one or more delicate, 6-petaled, star-shaped, blue-violet flowers. Blooms March-September.
Habitat: Moist areas in woodlands and meadows.
Comments: Related to popular ornamentals including freesias and gladiolas.

FRINGED GENTIAN
Gentianopsis detonsa
Size: To 15 in. (38 cm)
Description: Beautiful blue-violet, bell-shaped flowers have delicately fringed edges. Blooms in summer.
Habitat: Moist areas in the foothills and mountains.
Comments: Often cultivated as an ornamental.

WILD BLUE FLAX
Linum perenne
Size: To 2 ft. (60 cm)
Description: Wiry plant has narrow, slightly hairy, grass-like leaves. Purple to blue, 5-petalled flowers bloom in June-July.
Habitat: Dry slopes, sandy soils.
Comments: Tough stems were once used for weaving ropes and cloth. Seeds are a source of linseed oil.

TEASEL
Dipsacus sylvestris
Size: To 7 ft. (2.1 m)
Description: Prickly plant with a spikey purple flower head. Grass-like, erect leaves are also prickly on their undersides. Blooms April-September.
Habitat: Moist soils, fields, open woodlands.
Comments: Related to the garden variety pincushions.

ARIZONA REGIONS

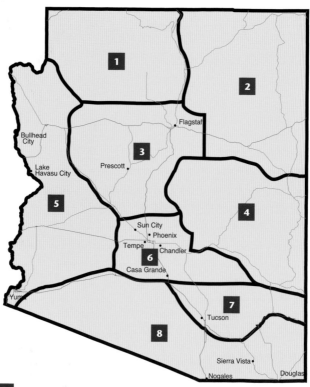

1 CANYON COUNTRY

2 INDIAN COUNTRY

3 CENTRAL TERRITORY

4 HIGH COUNTRY

5 WESTERN ARIZONA

6 PHOENIX AND VICINITY

7 TUCSON AND VICINITY

8 SOUTHERN ARIZONA

A land of extremes, Arizona's diverse landscape supports habitats that harbor a spectacular array of life. The Grand Canyon alone encompasses 5 of the 7 designated life zones found in North America. Dozens of parks, reserves, wildlife refuges and sanctuaries throughout the state protect and showcase the plant and animal life found here.

We have divided Arizona into 8 regions that generally reflect the state tourism regions.

1 CANYON COUNTRY

The spectacular Grand Canyon is the showpiece of this part of the state, and is one of many breathtaking attractions found here. The area is a popular vacation destination for tourists, riverrunners, fishermen, artisans and skiers, and draws nearly 4 million visitors a year.

2 INDIAN COUNTRY

The northeastern part of the state encompasses the Hopi and Navajo reservations, and is renowned for its natural and cultural attractions. Deep canyons, sacred mountains, petrified forests and towering monoliths of multi-hued rock are set in a mesmerizing landscape that continually changes color as the sun travels across the sky.

3 CENTRAL TERRITORY

This diverse part of the state encompasses grasslands, foothills, canyon and mountain habitats where modern cowboys and miners co-exist as they have for more than a century. The towns of Flagstaff and Williams, both gateways to the Grand Canyon, are set in the world's largest native stand of ponderosa pine.

4 HIGH COUNTRY

This alpine oasis serves as a summer retreat from the heat, and is a year-round recreational paradise. Boating, fishing, hiking, camping, climbing, snowmobiling, alpine skiing and even ice-fishing are a few of the attractions that keep drawing people back year after year.

5 WESTERN ARIZONA

The string of massive, well-stocked lakes on Arizona's western border make this one of the most popular watersports destinations in the U.S. A series of National Wildlife Refuges provide safe havens for hundreds of thousands of birds throughout the year.

6 PHOENIX AND VICINITY

Surrounded by a spectacular desert landscape, this populated region is a noted vacation destination for 'snowbirds' from the cooler parts of the country. Called the valley of the sun, the area averages over 330 sunny days a year. The area's plant and animal sanctuaries are world famous.

7 TUCSON AND VICINITY

Two of the gems in Arizona's crown are the Arizona-Sonora Desert Museum and the Saguaro National Park located near Tucson. The rugged Santa Catalina and Rincon Mountains provide a dramatic backdrop to the desert environment.

8 SOUTHERN ARIZONA

This classic country is the stuff of cowboy legends – a starkly beautiful, yet often forbidding landscape. A number of national monuments and wildlife refuges protect the delicate balance of desert life throughout this region. The region also features a number of lush wetland habitats that harbor a diversity of wildlife.

CANYON COUNTRY

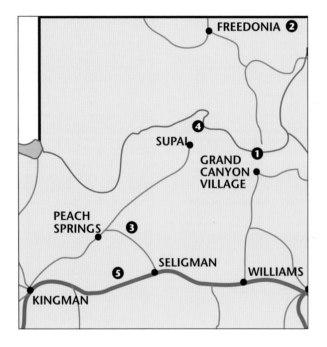

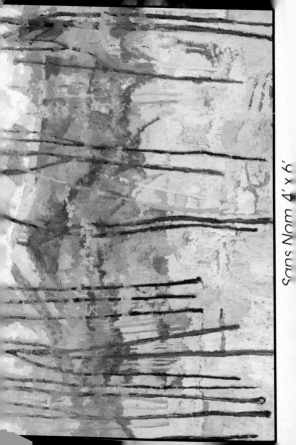

Sans Nom 4' x 6'

first sight.

So far their fine art paintings, sculpture, ceramics, up-cycled decor, design, wearables and library table of both old and new Taos art books, plus Jones' painting/demo studio, are stirring Taos creatives' pot and promising more Taos magic for years to come.

For more information, contact (575) 758-7965 or see *joneswalkeroftaos.com.* Jones Walker of Taos has a caveat for all – "You reap what you sow."

So far their fine art paintings, sculpture, ceramics, up-cycled decor, design, wearables and library table of both old and new Taos art books, plus Jones' painting/demo studio, are all stirring Taos creatives' pot and promising more Taos magic for years to come. ♦

For more information, contact (575) 758-7965 or see *joneswalkeroftaos.com.*

Clockwise: 'En La Sombra,' ...

Parks/Wildlife Areas

❶ GRAND CANYON NATIONAL PARK

One of the world's seven natural wonders, the Grand Canyon is the state's most popular natural attraction. Two billion years in the making, the canyon is 277 miles long and up to a mile deep. Words hardly do justice to the beauty and grandeur of the area. Perhaps John Muir put it best when he wrote, "No matter how far you have wandered . . . the Grand Canyon will seem as novel to you, as unearthly in its color and grandeur and the quantity of its architecture, as if you had found it after death, on some other star . . ."

Visitors can hike or ride mules to the bottom of the canyon (see hike #1 – page 151). Scenic bus and air tours, and rafting trips on the river are also popular ways to experience the unique environment. The easily accessible South Rim of the canyon is open year-round and attracts the large majority of tourists; the less-developed but equally spectacular North Rim is open mid-May to October (snows close the roads during winter). The South Rim features a full complement of services including a range of hotels, restaurants, shops, theaters, services and a large visitor center housing a museum and information center.

Accommodations and tours should be booked at least a year in advance. Campgrounds in the park should be booked several weeks in advance by calling (800) 365-2267. All back-country campers must obtain a permit from the Backcountry Office, Box 129, Grand Canyon, AZ, 86023.
Location: Grand Canyon Village
Phone: GCNPark (928) 638-7888
North Rim (928) 638-7864

N.B. – Anyone hiking into the canyon should be in good physical condition, wear sturdy footwear and carry a supply of water, food and warm clothing (even in summer).

❷ PARIA CANYON - VERMILLION CLIFFS WILDERNESS

Noted for its spectacular, twisting canyons elegantly sculpted from the colorful sandstone. Adventurous hikers can tackle the famous 37-mile-long canyon trail between Utah and Arizona. Hikers must register at one of the trailheads at White House, Buckskin, Wire Pass or Lee's Ferry.
Location: East of Page
Phone: (435) 688-3246

Museums/Attractions

❸ GRAND CANYON CAVERNS

Large underground limestone caverns are a popular attraction in summer. Guided tours take visitors 210 feet below the surface. Entrance features gift shop and small museum.
Location: Northwest of Seligman
Phone: (928) 422-3223

❹ HAVASU CANYON

Spectacular canyon adjoining the Grand Canyon features turquoise waterfalls, deep pools and lush orchards. The 8-mile hike to the canyon is arduous and should only be attempted by persons in good physical shape.
Location: Northeast of Peach Springs
Phone: (928) 448-2121

❺ AUBREY VALLEY

This area features an open grassland valley surrounded by 1,000-foot. cliffs. Noted for its hundreds of prairie dog towns, the area is also home to pronghorns, eagles and hawks.
Location: West of Seligman
Phone: (602) 942-3000

INDIAN COUNTRY

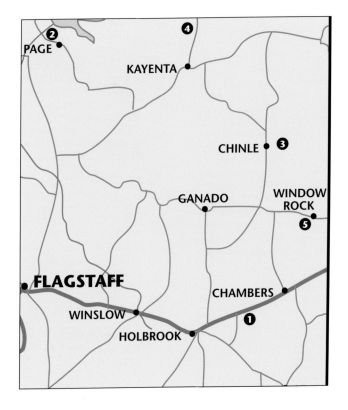

It is important to note that Indian Reservations in Arizona are considered private land; permits may be needed to camp, hike or travel off the main roads. Contact the Arizona Office of Tourism at 1-866-275-5816 for further information.

Parks/Wildlife Areas

❶ PETRIFIED FOREST NATIONAL PARK
Rare 'stone' trees, 225 million year-old fossilized logs, are scattered throughout this 100,000-acre park. Once the bottom of an ancient sea, the area is a world-famous source of fossils. Two visitor centers, a museum, interpretive trails and a self-guided, scenic drive highlight the park's unusual past. Inside the park boundaries are portions of the Painted Desert, a beautiful, strange, landscape of multi-colored, rolling mesas and plains that glow with each sunset.
Location: East of Holbrook
Phone: (520) 524-6228

❷ GLEN CANYON NATIONAL RECREATION AREA
Glen Canyon Dam impounds the second-largest artificial lake in the U.S., the 180-mile-long Lake Powell. Very few roads access the lake, so many visitors hike or boat their way in to experience the awesome canyon landscape. The highlight of the lake is a spectacular natural rock span – **Rainbow Bridge** – the world's largest, nearly 300 ft. wide and 300 ft. high. Located in Utah, most people reach the monument via boat from marinas in Arizona's Glen Canyon National Recreation Area. The site can also be reached via 2 hiking trails (26-30 miles round trip), but hiking permits must first be obtained from the Navajo Nation in Window Rock.
Location: Page
Phone: (928) 608-6404

❸ CANYON DE CHELLY NATIONAL MONUMENT
83,000-acre monument contains more than 100 miles of steep-walled, secluded canyons. Famous for its prehistoric ruins once occupied by nomadic Indians and the abundant pictographs etched into the canyon walls. Canyon de Chelly (pronounced "d-SHAY") and the adjoining Canyon del Muerto each have scenic rim roads with viewpoints along the edges. Guided hiking, driving and horseback-riding tours of the canyons are available.
Location: Near Chinle
Phone: (928) 674-5501

❹ MONUMENT VALLEY NAVAJO TRIBAL PARK
This colorful valley of towering sandstone monuments and eroded buttes has been a popular location for movies and commercials since the movie *Stagecoach* was filmed here in 1938. Area features scenic drives, tours, a museum and visitor center. Is near Four Corners, where Arizona, Utah, Colorado and New Mexico meet.
Location: Visitor center is north of Kayenta
Phone: (435) 727-5871

Museums/Attractions

❺ WINDOW ROCK
This mountain-with-a-hole-in-it is a famous landmark and a sacred ceremonial site for the Navajo. The nearby town of Window Rock is the capital of the Navajo Nation and the site of the world's largest American Indian Fair every September. The town features a zoological and botanical park that highlights native plants and animals.
Location: Window Rock
Phone: (928) 871-6000

CENTRAL TERRITORY

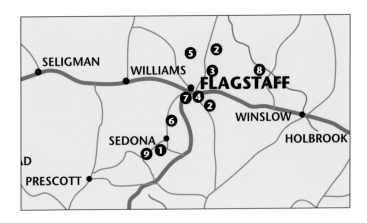

Parks/Wildlife Areas

① RED ROCK STATE PARK

Riparian system abounds with wildlife. Activities include bird walks and nature hikes. Visitor center highlights the ecology of Oak Creek. Look for bald eagles in winter. Spectacular views make it an ideal day-hike location.
Location: SW of Sedona
Phone: (928) 282-6907

② WUPATKI/WALNUT CANYON NATIONAL MONUMENTS

Both are sites of prehistoric Indian dwellings. Wupatki features the ruins of more than 800 rock dwellings; Walnut Canyon features 300 cliff dwellings. Each has a visitor center with displays, maps and books that discuss the human and natural history of each area.
Location: Wupatki; 35 mi. NE of Flagstaff
Phone: (928) 679-2365
Location: Walnut Canyon; 10 mi. SE of Flagstaff
Phone: (928) 526-3367

③ SUNSET CRATER VOLCANO NATIONAL MONUMENT

The remnant of a volcanic eruption, this striking, black cinder cone rises more than 1,000 feet above a moon-like landscape of lava flows. Area features visitor center, self-guided trails, picnic and camping areas.
Location: 15 mi. north of Flagstaff
Phone: (928) 526-0502

Museums/Attractions

④ MUSEUM OF NORTHERN ARIZONA

Features excellent displays on the natural and human history of northern Arizona.
Location: Flagstaff
Phone: (928) 774-5211

⑤ SAN FRANCISCO PEAKS

Arizona's tallest mountains are part of a vast field of cinder cones, volcanic peaks and lava flows that cover 3,000 square miles. Abundant trails make the peaks an ideal day-hike destination. The area also features the Lamar Haines Wildlife Area, a noted birding spot.
Location: North of Flagstaff
Phone: (928) 526-0866

⑥ OAK CREEK CANYON

A renowned, accessible canyon featuring huge rock monoliths, rocky gorges and dramatic red, white and yellow cliffs dotted with cypresses and junipers. Within the canyon boundaries is Slide Rock State Park, noted for its natural rock water slide.
Location: North of Sedona
Phone: (928) 282-7722

⑦ THE ARBORETUM

200-acre sanctuary highlights native and non-native flora that thrive in the cooler Flagstaff climate. Phone for hours and tour information.
Location: Flagstaff
Phone: (928) 774-1442

⑧ GRAND FALLS

Spectacular 185-foot (56 m) falls are higher than Niagara Falls. Best viewed after rainstorm or spring snowmelt.
Location: Northeast of Flagstaff
Phone: (602) 871-6647

⑨ PAGE SPRINGS FISH HATCHERY

Modern facility is designed to produce more than a million catchable trout per year. Visitor center features interpretive exhibits that are complemented by an outdoor nature trail and wildlife watching area.
Location: 12 mi. south of Sedona
Phone: (928) 634-4805

HIGH COUNTRY

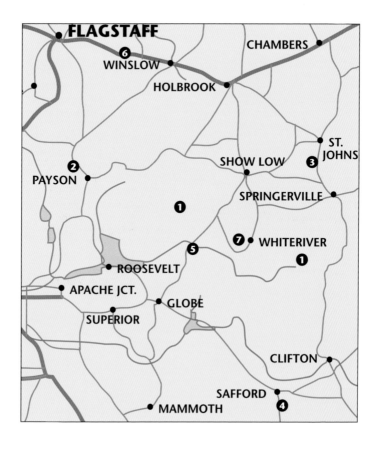

Parks/Wildlife Areas

1 WHITE MOUNTAIN APACHE INDIAN RESERVATION

This reservation has well-developed recreation facilities and is considered one of the state's premier attractions for sporting enthusiasts. A fisherman's paradise, the area has 26 lakes and hundreds of miles of productive trout streams. Quality hiking, camping, boating and fishing destinations are scattered throughout the reservation's 1.6 million acres. Tribal permits are required for most activities.
Location: East-central Arizona
Phone: (928) 338-4346

2 TONTO NATURAL BRIDGE STATE PARK

Area is site of the world's largest travertine (limestone) bridge – over 400 ft. long and 183 ft. high. Popular hiking and picnicking area.
Location: Northwest of Payson
Phone: (928) 476-4202

3 LYMAN LAKE STATE PARK

High-country lake is a popular camping, fishing, hiking and water skiing location. More than 100 species of birds are found here, including bald eagles and osprey. Small herd of bison graze near park entrance.
Location: South of St. John's
Phone: (928) 337-4441

4 ROPER LAKE STATE PARK

A natural hot springs is the major attraction at this camping and picnicking haven.
Location: South of Safford
Phone: (928) 428-6760

Museums/Attractions

5 SALT RIVER CANYON

Deep canyon is noted for its spectacular vistas and is called the mini-Grand Canyon by some. Features multi-colored rock walls, spires buttes and mesas. Guided rafting trips are a popular way to experience the breathtaking scenery of the surrounding wilderness area.
Location: Hwy 60 crosses the canyon 33 mi. NE of Globe
Phone: (928) 425-7189

6 METEOR CRATER

Huge crater 570 ft. deep and nearly a mile wide was created when a gigantic meteor hit the earth at 33,000 mph. Considered to be one of the best-preserved craters in the world. Museum features educational displays and a 1,400 lb. meteorite.
Location: 40 mi. east of Flagstaff
Phone: (928) 289-2362

7 WILLIAMS CREEK AND ALCHESAY NATIONAL FISH HATCHERIES

Both raise species of trout for distribution to Indian Reservations. Williams Creek is the center for the culture and distribution of Arizona's threatened state fish – the Apache trout. Each features interpretive information and are popular picnicking and fishing destinations.
Location: Whiteriver
Phone: WC (928) 334-2346
Alchesay (928) 338-4901

WESTERN ARIZONA

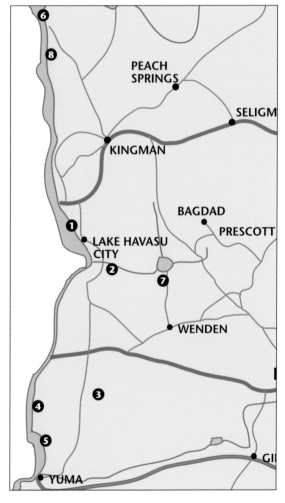

PEACH
SPRINGS

SELIGM

KINGMAN

BAGDAD

PRESCOTT

LAKE HAVASU
CITY

WENDEN

GI

YUMA

Parks/Wildlife Areas

NATIONAL WILDLIFE REFUGES (NWR)

A series of refuges along Arizona's western border offer excellent wildlife viewing opportunities. The marshes, lakes and adjacent desert support a vast array of resident birds and tens of thousands of migratory waterfowl in winter.

❶ HAVASU NWR

Marshes, open water and desert habitats attract a variety of waterfowl and some neotropical birds. Highlights are Topcock Gorge, a spectacular steep-walled canyon, and one of the last stretches of virgin river in the state.
Location: Refuge headquarters is in Needles, CA.
Phone: (760) 326-3853

❷ BILL WILLIAMS NWR

Marshlands and lush cottonwood-willow forests attract a vast diversity of wildlife.
Location: South of Quartzsite
Phone: (928) 667-4144

❸ KOFA NWR

This rugged mountain refuge protects more than 800 bighorn sheep and the state's most noted grove of native palm trees. Coyotes, rabbits, foxes and desert birds are also common.
Location: 28 mi. NE of Parker
Phone: (602) 783-7861

❹ CIBOLA NWR

Refuge includes marshland, desert, river, backwater lakes and ponds. Has largest populations of geese and sandhill cranes on the lower Colorado River.
Location: Accessed via Hwy 10 west of Blythe, CA
Phone: (928) 857-3253

❺ IMPERIAL NWR

Habitats include marshes, ponds, backwater lakes and desert. Popular area for fishing and birding.
Location: Northwest of Yuma
Phone: (928) 783-3371

❻ LAKE MEAD NATIONAL RECREATION AREA

Two lakes over 170 miles in length create a boater's and angler's paradise in northwestern Arizona. The northern Lake Mead, created by the famous Hoover Dam, is the largest artificial lake in the U.S. and has more than 800 miles of shoreline. The smaller Lake Mohave was created by the Davis Dam. The lakes are both well-stocked by hatcheries and each features dozens of sandy beaches and secluded coves for camping, swimming and picnicking.
Location: Northwest Arizona
Phone: Lake Mead: (702) 293-8907
Lake Mohave: (702) 293-8990

❼ ALAMO LAKE STATE PARK

Located in a transition zone between the Mohave and Sonoran deserts, the lake and surrounding area sup-port a diversity of plants and animals. A popular recreational destination noted for its excellent fishing.
Location: 38 mi. north of Wenden
Phone: (928) 669-2088

Museums/Attractions

❽ WILLOW BEACH NATIONAL FISH HATCHERY

Hatchery raises a huge population of trout for stocking Lake Mohave and also studies the propagation of endangered local species. Displays and outdoor raceways highlight fish behavior.
Location: South of the Hoover Dam
Phone: (928) 767-3456

PHOENIX AND VICINITY

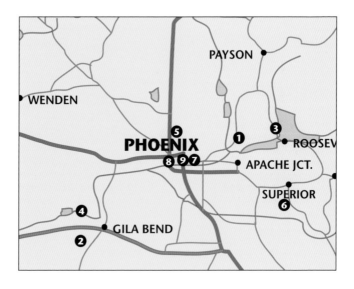

Parks/Wildlife Areas

❶ LOST DUTCHMAN STATE PARK
This popular camping, hiking and wildlife viewing destination is located at the base of the famous Superstition Mountains. The park features short nature trails, and several well-marked trails lead into the rugged Superstition Mountains Wilderness Area.
Location: 5 mi. northeast of Apache Junction
Phone: (602) 542-4174

❷ ROBBINS BUTTE WILDLIFE AREA
A haven for doves, the area attracts a wide variety of bird species including raptors, quail and songbirds. Rattlesnakes and the rare Gila monster may be spotted in summer.
Location: 40 mi. SW of Phoenix
Phone: (480) 981-9400

❸ ROOSEVELT LAKE WILDLIFE AREA
Reservoir created by Roosevelt Dam attracts abundant bird life, including bald eagles, osprey and waterfowl.
Location: Near Roosevelt
Phone: (480) 981-9400

❹ PAINTED ROCK STATE PARK
Area has abundant avian and reptilian wildlife, including cactus wrens, turkey vultures, raptors, chuckwallas, Gila monsters and whiptails. Named for the prehistoric pictures, petroglyphs, found etched on hundreds of rocks.
Location: West of Gila Bend
Phone: (623) 580-5500

❺ NORTH MOUNTAIN PARK
Nature trails wind through 7,000 acres of the Phoenix Mountain Preserve. Guided trail rides are available.
Location: Phoenix
Phone: (602) 262-7901

Museums/Attractions

❻ BOYCE THOMPSON ARBORETUM
Outstanding 1,000-acre sanctuary features more than 1,500 species of hot-weather plants from around the world. More than 240 species of animals can be spotted among the plants. Miles of trails wind through the 35-acre site of this noted botanical garden and research center.
Location: Near Superior
Phone: (520) 689-2811

❼ DESERT BOTANICAL GARDEN
Pathways meander through a natural desert setting. More than 2,000 species of desert plants from around the world are featured, including the unusual boojum tree. A 3-acre exhibit highlights natural communities including a saguaro forest, mesquite thicket, desert stream and upland chaparral. Garden also provides information on the location of important wildflower blooms throughout the state.
Location: Phoenix
Phone: (480) 481-8134

❽ PHOENIX ZOO
The largest privately owned zoo in the U.S., it accommodates more than 1,300 local and exotic animals and birds. The 125-acre zoo recreates various habitats from around the world including rainforests, grasslands, temperate forests and deserts.
Location: Phoenix
Phone: (602) 273-1341

❾ ARIZONA SCIENCE CENTER
Popular interactive museum features more than 100 exhibits on a variety of science-related topics.
Location: Phoenix
Phone: (602) 716-2000

TUCSON AND VICINITY

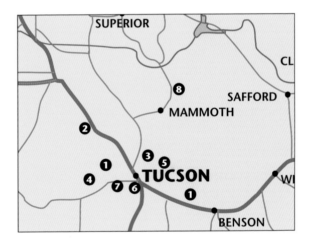

Parks/Wildlife Areas

❶ SAGUARO NATIONAL PARK

Divided into two sections by the city of Tucson, this park protects more than 83,000 acres of the Sonoran Desert. The towering 'armed' saguaro cactus dominates the landscape. Wildlife and bird watching, backcountry hiking and camping are popular activities. More than 75 miles of trails wind through habitats ranging from deserts to pine forests. The Rincon Mountain District of the park located east of Tucson is accessed via Old Spanish Trail; the western Tucson Mountain District is accessed via Speedway Boulevard. Each district has a visitor center that provides detailed information on trails and scenic drives. Petroglyphs can be viewed in the western district. There is an admission fee to the eastern district; the western district is free.
Location: Tucson
Phone: (520) 733-5153

❷ PICACHO PEAK STATE PARK

Park features a 1,500-foot sheer-sided peak that erupts from the desert floor. Is a noted location for desert study and spring wildflower displays.
Location: 40 miles NW of Tucson
Phone: (520) 466-3183

❸ CATALINA STATE PARK

5,500-acre park at the base of the Catalina Mountains is home to a variety of plant and animal life. Area is noted for its spectacular spring wildflower display. Nature study, camping, hiking and horseback riding are a few of the activities visitors can enjoy here.
Location: North of Tucson
Phone: (520) 628-5798

Museums/Attractions

❹ ARIZONA-SONORA DESERT MUSEUM

The state's second most popular tourist attraction is regarded as one of the finest museums in the world. Paths wind through indoor and outdoor exhibits where several hundred species of desert animals and plants can be viewed up close in their natural environment. Other exhibits include dioramas, native gardens, aquariums and an earth-sciences center.
Location: West of Tucson
Phone: (520) 883-2702

❺ SABINO CANYON

Scenic canyon in the Santa Catalina Mountains features numerous trails, waterfalls and a visitor center. One of the most popular retreats near Tucson.
Location: East of Tucson
Phone: (520) 749-2861

❻ TUCSON BOTANICAL GARDENS

Self-guided trails wind through 5 acres of gardens highlighting species from arid, semi-arid and tropical environments.
Location: Tucson
Phone: (520) 326-9686

❼ INTERNATIONAL WILDLIFE MUSEUM

Excellent dioramas and displays feature hundreds of mounted animals and birds from around the world.
Location: 7 mi. west of Tucson
Phone: (520) 617-1439

❽ ARAVAIPA CANYON

Lush 7.5-mile-long canyon is noted for its spectacular scenery and abundant wildlife. There is no vehicle access, and permits to hike the canyon must be obtained well in advance.
Location: Northeast of Mammoth
Phone: (928) 348-4400

SOUTHERN ARIZONA

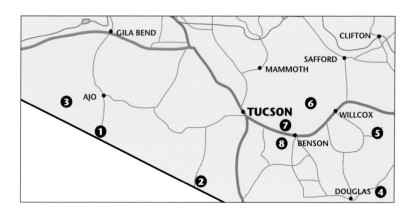

Parks/Wildlife Areas

❶ ORGAN PIPE CACTUS NATIONAL MONUMENT

A showcase of the native plants and animals of the Sonoran Desert, including the rare organ pipe cactus. Often the setting for wondrous wildflower blooms February-April (weather permitting). Self-guided nature trails and scenic drives are popular activities. The endangered desert pupfish can be found in Quitobaquito Spring. Visitor center has excellent information on the common plants and animals.
Location: 22 mi. south of Why
Phone: (520) 387-6849

❷ BUENOS AIRES NATIONAL WILDLIFE REFUGE

More than 230 bird species have been identified in this refuge featuring rare cienegas (wetlands) riparian woodlands, and a mountain canyon. Also has largest ungrazed grassland in the state.
Location: Southwest of Tucson
Phone: (520) 823-4251

❸ CABEZA PRIETA NATIONAL WILDLIFE REFUGE

This 860,000-acre refuge in the Sonoran Desert harbors desert bighorn sheep, pronghorn, mule deer and a host of reptiles and birds. Entry permits must be obtained from the Visitor Center in Ajo before entering.
Location: West of Ajo
Phone: (520) 387-6483

❹ SAN BERNADINO/LESLIE CANYON NATIONAL WILDLIFE REFUGE

Located near the Mexican border, the area is one of the best birding spots in the country. Habitats include lush riparian systems, mesquite bosque and desert grasslands. Visitors are required to obtain entry permits from the refuge office in Douglas at 1408 10th St.
Location: Near Douglas
Phone: (520) 364-2104

❺ CHIRICAHUA NATIONAL MONUMENT

A spectacular, rocky wilderness, known for its huge balanced rocks, towering spires and stone columns. Locals call it the "Land of Standing-Up Rocks." The forests harbor unusual wildlife species including the raccoon-like coati and pig-like javelina.
Location: Near Willcox
Phone: (520) 824-3560, Ext. 104

❻ MULESHOE RANCH MANAGEMENT AREA

The area contains a variety of habitats from deserts to pine forests. It is a haven for five species of fish, including the endangered Gila Chub. There are more than 200 bird species and mammals such as the javelina and coati. Accommodations are limited and should be booked well in advance.
Location: Northwest of Willcox
Phone: (520) 586-7072

Museums/Attractions

❼ COLOSSAL CAVE

The largest dry cave in the world, it was used by desperadoes as a hideout. Guided tours, gift shop and snack bar.
Location: 22 mi. east of Tucson
Phone: (520) 647-7275

❽ KARTCHNER CAVERNS STATE PARK

A pristine limestone cave has two rooms the size of football fields.
Location: 16 mi. south of Benson
Phone: (520) 586-4100

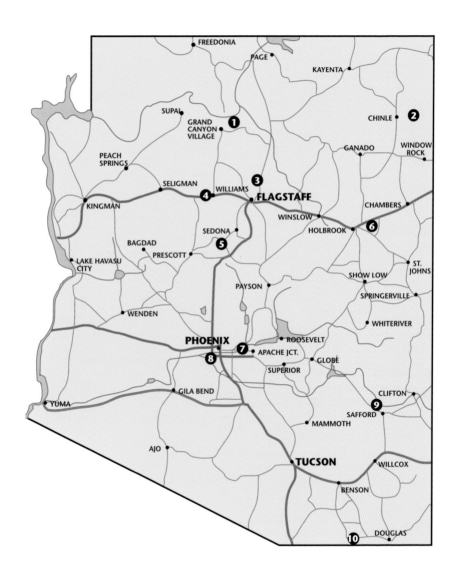

10 HIKES

1 **BRIGHT ANGEL TRAIL 15.6 mi.* (25 km)**
One of America's most famous hikes, it descends 4,000 ft. (1,219 m) into the
Grand Canyon. Two key things to remember: 1) It is easier to hike in than out;
and 2) Mules have the right of way. (928) 638-7888.†

2 **WHITE HOUSE RUIN TRAIL 2 mi. (3.2 km)**
Trail along the rim of Canyon de Chelley offers views of the area's well-known
cliff dwellings. Is the only trail in the area that can be hiked without a permit.
(928) 674-5501.

3 **HUMPHREY'S TRAIL 9 mi. (14.4 km)**
Trail leads to the highest point in Arizona atop Humphrey's Peak at 12,633 ft.
(3,850 m). Elevation gain along the route is 1,300 ft. (396 m).
(928) 526-0866.

4 **BILL WILLIAMS TRAIL 6 mi. (9.6 km)**
Trail through pine forests leads to summit of Bill Williams Mountain and offers a
view of the North Rim of the Grand Canyon. (928) 635-4061.

5 **GENERAL CROOK TRAIL 272 mi. (438 km)**
This National Recreation Trail follows the route between forts Apache and
Whipple established in the 19th century. Part of the trail follows the Mogollon
Rim and offers spectacular views of the area. (928) 567-4121.

6 **CRYSTAL FOREST TRAIL .8 mi. (1.3 km)**
Easy hike along paved pathway past petrified trees. (928) 524-6228.

7 **DUTCHMAN'S TRAIL 36.4 mi. (58.4 km)**
Popular trail leads into the Superstition Mountains and connects with numerous
other trails. Highlight is a view of a 4,500 ft. (1,371 m) volcanic plug, Weaver's
Needle. (602) 225-5200.

8 **SUN CIRCLE TRAIL 8 mi. (12.9 km)**
Trail near Phoenix offers panoramic views of the city and surrounding area.
Highlights include unusual geologic formations. A National Recreation Trail.
(602) 506-2930.

9 **SAFFORD-MORENCI TRAIL 30 mi. (48 km)**
Popular winding trail through canyons in the Turtle and Gila mountains.
Highlights include early homestead sites, cliff dwellings and huge rocky
outcrops. (928) 348-4400.

10 **ARIZONA TRAIL 800 mi. (1280 km)**
The Arizona Trail extends from the Coronado National Monument at the US-
Mexico border and extends north all the way to the Kaibab Plateau region at the
Arizona-Utah state line. It is designed as a primitive trail for hikers, bikers and
cross-country skiers. (602) 542-7120.

* All distances are for return trips.
† Call for more information.

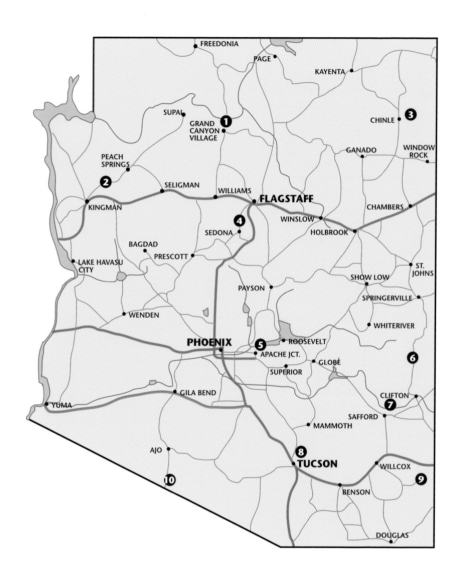

10 SCENIC DRIVES

1 **GRAND CANYON – EAST RIM** 25 mi.* (40 km)
Popular drive from Grand Canyon Village to Desert Watchtower passes several
overlooks including the famous Grandview Point. (928) 638-7888.†

2 **HISTORIC ROUTE 66** 140 mi. (225 km)
The longest existing stretch of America's first transcontinental highway winds
through the Black Mountain range. Route begins west of Ashfork and leads
through Seligman, Peach Springs, Kingman and Oatman to Topcock. Highway
is called the 'Main Street of America.' (928) 753-5001.

3 **CANYON DE CHELLY – SOUTH RIM** 18 mi. (29 km)
Scenic route has several overlooks of towering cliffs, canyons and ruins.
Highlights are Spider Rock and White House Ruin. (928) 674-5501.

4 **OAK CREEK CANYON** 88 mi. loop (142 km)
Winding scenic highway through stunning canyon with white, yellow and red
cliffs and unusual rock formations. (928) 282-7722.

5 **APACHE TRAIL** 39 mi. (63 km)
Originally an ancient route of the Apache Indians through the Salt River
canyons, it was converted to a roadway in 1905 to transport supplies for
the construction of the Roosevelt Dam. Paved/dirt road passes through
spectacular scenery. (602) 364-3700.

6 **CORONADO TRAIL** 123 mi. (198 km)
Scenic highway between Springerville and Clifton descends more than a mile
between mountain and desert habitats. Excellent wildlife viewing opportunities.
Parallels the route followed by Francisco Vasquez de Coronado when he sought
the fabled Seven Cities of Cibola in the 16th century. (602) 364-3700.

7 **BLACK HILLS NATIONAL BACK COUNTRY BYWAY** 21 mi. (34 km)
Unpaved road leads into the spectacular Gila Box Riparian National
Conservation Area. (928) 348-4400.

8 **MOUNT LEMMON SCENIC DRIVE** 24 mi. (39 km)
The General Hitchcock Highway (also called the Catalina Highway), travels
through a series of life zones as it climbs from the desert floor to an alpine environment. Wildlife is abundant and diverse in each zone. A few parking areas
feature interpretive information, and there is a small ski area and
restaurant at the top. (520) 749-8700.

9 **CHIRICAHUA NATIONAL MONUMENT DRIVE** 36mi. (58 km)
Scenic route from Willcox via state highways 186 and 181 winds through
grassland and forested habitats. Wildlife is unusual and abundant.
(520) 824-3560.

10 **PUERTO BLANCO DRIVE** 52 mi. (84 km)
Dirt road through Organ Pipe Cactus National Monument highlights its virgin
desert habitat and unique plants and animals. Drive is infrequently closed by
rain. (520) 387-6849.

* All distances are for one-way trips unless otherwise indicated.
† Call for more information.

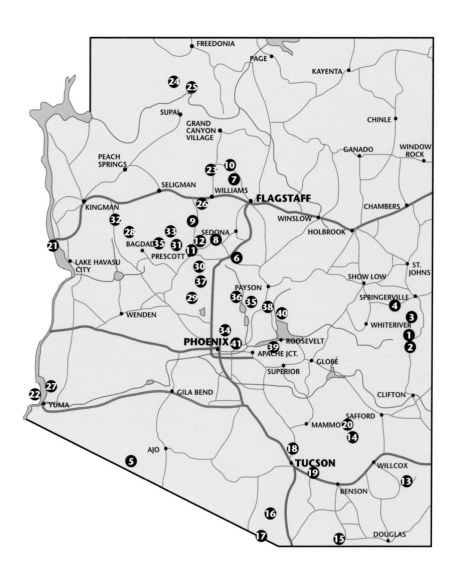

ARIZONA NATIONAL FORESTS & WILDERNESS AREAS

There are a number of wilderness areas in Arizona that preserve the landscape in an undisturbed state. Most are roadless and are only open to visitors on foot or horseback. Visitors should contact the area office regarding backcountry permits and seasonal information and maps before proceeding.

Apache-Sitgreaves National Forest Wilderness Areas
309 S. Mountain Avenue, P.O. Box 640, Springerville, AZ 85938
(602) 333-4301
The Apache-Sitgreaves National Forests encompass habitats including mixed woodlands (pinyon-juniper, ponderosa pine, mixed conifer and spruce-fir) and desert. One of the wettest places in Arizona, it features 2 dozen lakes and reservoirs and more than 400 miles of waterways, and is a popular recreation destination. The ample water acts like a magnet for wildlife, and more than 410 species make their home here.

❶ Bear Wallow Wilderness Area
Size: 11,080 acres (4,484 ha)
Features one of the Southwest's largest virgin stands of ponderosa pine. Wildlife is abundant, and Bear Wallow Creek harbors native Apache trout. Trail at south of area leads to the top of the Mogollon Rim.

❷ Blue Range Primitive Area
Size: 29,304 acres (11,859 ha)
Scenic attractions include the Mogollon Rim and the magnificent Blue River Canyon and river. Spruce, pine and fir forests provide food and shelter for deer and elk. Trail access is good.

❸ Escudilla Wilderness Area
Size: 5,200 acres (2,104 ha)
Located atop the 10,000-foot Escudilla Mountain, the area is famous for its vistas and mountain meadows.

❹ Mt. Baldy Wilderness Area
Size: 7,000 acres (2,832 ha)
Two popular trails lead into the wilderness and join each other atop Mt. Baldy. The Mt. Baldy summit is on the Fort Apache Indian Reservation and is closed to the public. Area features deep canyons and miles of fishing streams. The area is very popular, and because of its small size, group limits have been imposed. Hiking groups should not exceed 12 individuals, and overnight camping groups should not exceed 6. Permits are not required to enter the area.

❺ Cabeza Prieta Wilderness Area
1611 N. 2nd Ave. Ajo, AZ (520) 387-6483
Size: 803,418 acres (325,143 ha)
The Cabeza Prieta National Wildlife Refuge became a designated wilderness area in 1990. The desert area features low mountain ranges and broad valleys. Bighorn sheep are abundant. Area is noted for its spring wildflower displays.

Coconino National Forest Wilderness Areas

2323 E. Greenlaw Lane, Flagstaff, Arizona 86004 (928) 527-3600
The Coconino National Forest encompasses the spectacular volcanic San Francisco peaks, Oak Creek Canyon and part of the towering Mogollon Rim. Elevations range from 2,600-12,600 feet. Considered by many to be the finest wooded area in the state. Big-game species include elk, deer, pronghorn, bear, turkey and mountain lion.

➏ Fossil Springs Wilderness Area

Size: 11,550 acres (4,674 ha)
Natural springs found within a deep, steep-walled canyon create a lush riparian habitat within the surrounding desert scrub. Dozens of species of trees and hundreds of species of animals live in the diverse niches found here. A noted, pristine wilderness area.

➐ Kachina Peaks Wilderness Area

Size: 18,616 acres (7,534 ha)
One of the highest wilderness areas in Arizona, it supports the state's only arctic-alpine habitat. Because of the fragility of the area, visitors must stay on designated trails and camping is not allowed above the timberline. Also note that local Indian tribes have erected some religious shrines within the area that are currently in use and should not be disturbed. Elevations range between 7,400-12,600 feet.

➑ Munds Mountain Wilderness Area

Size: 24,411 acres (9,879 ha)
Characterized by unique red rock formations, this area is a popular hiking, camping, rock-climbing and birding destination. Variable woodland and riparian habitats harbor a diverse array of plant and animal species. Elevations range from 3,600-6,800 feet.

➒ Red Rock - Secret Mountain Wilderness Area

Size: 47,194 acres (19,099 ha)
Area is characterized by spectacular colored cliffs, deep canyons and high mesas. Diverse vegetation of the area supports more than 250 species of vertebrates, including elk, mountain lions and javelina.

➓ Strawberry Crater Wilderness Area

Size: 10,743 acres (4,348 ha)
Part of the San Francisco Mountain volcanic field, the area is dominated by volcanic rugged lava flows, cinder cones and craters. A popular day-hiking and backpacking location, it offer excellent views of the Painted Desert and the surrounding area. Elevations range from 5,500-6,000 feet.

⑪ West Clear Creek Wilderness Area
Size: 15,238 acres (6,167 ha)
Remote area features the longest canyon that cuts through the Mogollon Rim.
A number of good trails lead to the canyon bottom, and experienced hikers will
enjoy traversing the wild depths of the entire canyon.

⑫ Wet Beaver Wilderness Area
Size: 6,155 acres (2,490 ha)
Area features lush riparian habitat set in a steep, red-walled, twisting canyon.
One of the few areas in the state with a perennial, flowing desert stream.

Coronado National Forest Wilderness Areas
300 W. Congress St., Tucson, Arizona 85701 (520) 388-8300
The Coronado Forest covers several sections of desert and mountainous landscape in southern and southeastern Arizona. Its 1.7 million acres encompass 12
mountain ranges and a vast diversity of life zones found between elevations of
3,000 to 10,700 feet. In some areas, visitors can travel between desert to alpine
habitats in less than an hour.

⑬ Chiricahua Wilderness Area
Size: 87,700 acres (35,492 ha)
Variable area with steep slopes, deep canyons and dense cover provide habitats
for a diverse array of plant and animal life. A number of unusual Mexican bird
species are found here.

⑭ Galiuro Wilderness Area
Size: 76,317 acres (30,885 ha)
Rugged wilderness area features brightly colored cliffs and steep slopes.
Habitats including semi-desert grassland, mixed woodlands and extensive
riparian systems support an abundance of animals including deer, bear,
javelina, coati and mountain lion. Elevations range between 4,000-7,600 feet.

⑮ Miller Peak Wilderness Area
Size: 20,100 acres (8,134 ha)
This rugged area is a haven for hundreds of species of birds, reptiles and
mammals. Trails are well-maintained and lead to some of the most spectacular
viewpoints in the south. Miller Peak rises to an elevation of 9,466 feet.

⑯ Mount Wrightson Wilderness Area
Size: 25,200 acres (10,198 ha)
The 9,400 foot Mt. Wrightson is located in the heart of this rugged area.
Numerous stream-fed canyons support riparian systems and an abundance of
plants and animals, including a number of rare birds. Is an extremely popular,
internationally renowned birding destination.

⑰ Pajarita Wilderness Area
Size: 7,240 acres (2,930 ha)
Located on the Arizona/Mexico border, the area protects an important wildlife corridor. Plant and animal species from both sides of the border merge here, making it an extremely popular wildlife viewing area. Area noted for its spectacular wildflower displays.

⑱ Pusch Ridge Wilderness Area
Size: 56,900 acres (23,027 ha)
Adjacent to Tucson, this wilderness area ascends over 5,000 feet from the desert floor to the peaks of the Santa Catalina mountains. It encompasses several distinct life zones and a vast diversity of plants and animals. Trail system is extensive and area is easily accessed. Elevations range from 2,800-9,000 feet.

⑲ Rincon Mountain Wilderness Area
Size: 38,600 acres (15,621 ha)
Mountain wilderness protects three sides of Saguaro National Park. Well-marked trails wind through the area and into the national park. Access to the area is via Forest Road 35. Terrain is rocky and steep and back-country hikers should exercise extreme caution. Elevations range from 3,600-7,700 feet.

⑳ Santa Teresa Wilderness Area
Size: 28,780 acres (11,647 ha)
Area is characterized by rugged mountain terrain, large canyons and mesas. Elevations range from 4,000-7,500 feet. There are a number of good trails, although road access to the area is over rough unpaved roads.

㉑ Havasu Wilderness Area
P.O. Box 3009, Needles, CA 92363 (760) 326-3853
Size: 14,600 acres (5,908 ha)
Located within the Havasu National Wildlife Refuge, the area's desert and mountain habitats support abundant plant and animal life. Note that summer temperatures can be exceedingly hot.

㉒ Imperial Wilderness Area
P.O. Box 72217, Martinez Lake, AZ 85365 (928) 783-3371
Size: 9,200 acres (3,723 ha)
Located within the Imperial National Wildlife Refuge, it encompasses some of the hottest territory in the country. The adjoining Colorado River provides a riparian habitat which supports desert bighorn sheep, the rare desert tortoise and abundant bird life. Elevations range from 200-2,800 feet.

Kaibab National Forest Wilderness Areas
800 South 6th St., Williams, Arizona 86046 (928) 635-4061
The Kaibab National Forest skirts both sides of the Grand Canyon and the northern part of the San Francisco Peaks and ranges in elevation from 5,500-10,400 feet. Habitats range from desert to alpine and each has its own characteristic species. Access in spring can be limited due to snowmelt and runoff.

㉓ Kendrick Mountain Wilderness Area
Size: 7,300 acres (2,954 ha)
Area protects a remnant of the San Francisco Mountain volcanic field. The mountain is over 10,000 feet tall and supports coniferous forests and mixed woods. The varying slopes of the mountain provide important habitats for birds and mammals. Trails are well-maintained and offer spectacular vistas. Vehicles are prohibited. Located in both the Kaibab and Coconino National Forests.

㉔ Kanab Creek Wilderness Area
Size: 68,250 acres (27,620 ha)
This area protects Kanab Creek, one of the major tributaries of the Colorado River. The creek's tributaries have carved deep gorges and fantastic shapes and forms into the surrounding plateaus. Access is difficult and trails are poorly marked. Area is extremely hot in summer. Elevations range from 2,000-6,000 feet.

㉕ Saddle Mountain Wilderness Area
Size: 40,600 acres (16,430 ha)
Bounded on 3 sides by deep canyons, this area was named for a prominent ridge that closely resembles a saddle. Terrain is rocky and steep and difficult to navigate, but the panoramic views, trophy deer, apache trout and remnant herd of bison make a visit well worth the effort. Elevations range from 6,000-8,000 feet.

㉖ Sycamore Canyon Wilderness Area
Size: 56,000 acres (22,663 ha)
Noted for its deep winding canyon and spectacular red and white cliffs. Vehicles are prohibited. The area is shared by 3 national forests – the Prescott, Kaibab and Coconino.

㉗ Kofa Wilderness Area
W. First St., P.O. Box 6290, Yuma, AZ 85366-6290 (928) 783-7861
Size: 516,000 acres (208,825 ha)
Located within the Kofa National Wildlife Refuge, the area features 2 mountain ranges and a broad valley. Climate is hot with little annual precipitation. Desert bighorn sheep are abundant, and the area has the state's most notable grove of native fan palms. Hiking, camping and hunting are allowed.

Prescott National Forest Wilderness Areas
344 South Cortez Street, Prescott, Arizona 86303 (928) 443-8000
Prescott National Forest covers an area of almost 1.25 million acres in central Arizona. Habitats range from desert grasslands and chaparral to mixed wood-lands and pine forests. The area offers outstanding recreational opportunities year round, and is a very popular destination for residents and tourists alike.

28 **Apache Creek Wilderness Area**
Size: 5,240 acres (2,120 ha)
Rugged area features rolling hills, rocky outcrops, riparian (river and streamside) habitats and three natural springs.

29 **Castle Creek Wilderness Area**
Size: 29,750 acres (12,039 ha)
Very rugged area has granite peaks of up 7,000 feet in elevation. Grassland and chaparral habitats are found at lower elevations; mixed pine-oak forests dominate at upper elevations.

30 **Cedar Bench Wilderness Area**
Size: 14,840 acres (6,005 ha)
Area divides the Verde and Agua Fria drainages. Chaparral is the dominant habitat. Elevations range between 4,500-6,700 feet.

31 **Granite Mountain Wilderness Area**
Size: 9,700 acres (3,925 ha)
Area is noted for its giant stacked granite boulders that reach elevations of 7,500 feet.

32 **Juniper Mesa Wilderness Area**
Size: 7,600 acres (3,075 ha)
A large, flat-topped mesa dominates this wilderness area. Though no permanent water is found here, animals including squirrels and deer are relatively common. Trails and public access points are maintained.

33 **Woodchute Wilderness Area**
Size: 5,700 acres (2,306 ha)
Easily accessed wilderness area features maintained trails and offers spectacular views of central Arizona. Elevations range between 5,500-7,800 feet.

Tonto National Forest Wilderness Areas
2324 E. McDowell Road, P.O. Box 5348, Phoenix, Arizona 85010
(602) 225-5200
One of the country's largest forests, The Tonto National Forest encompasses nearly 3 million acres of desert and alpine habitats. The forest's 6 lakes and hundreds of miles of waterways create diverse ecosystems which support abundant and variable species. More than 400 species of vertebrates are found here. Scenic roadways include the Beeline Highway (SR 87), the Young Highway (SR 288) and the famous Apache Trail (SR 88).

34 **Four Peaks Wilderness**
Size: 53,500 acres (21,651 ha)
Wilderness area near Phoenix encompasses mountain and desert habitats. Named for 4 mountain peaks that are are visible for miles. Trail system is well-developed. Elevations range between 1,900-7,500 feet.

35 Hellsgate Wilderness Area
Size: 37,440 acres (15,151 ha)
Noted for its canyon and large stream that forms deep pools and scenic water-falls. Trails are limited.

36 Mazatzal Wilderness Area
Size: 252,000 acres (101,984 ha)
This rough, desert mountain wilderness is found in both the Tonto and Coconino National Forests. Arizona's only designated wild river, the Verde, flows through the region. Trail system is extensive and well-maintained. Elevations range from 1,600- 7,900 feet.

37 Pine Mt. Wilderness Area
Size: 20,100 acres (8,134 ha)
Located along the boundary between the Prescott and Tonto National Forests. Desert mountains surround this small island of primarily ponderosa pine forests. Hikers climb through several distinct life zones as they ascend to the top of the 6,800-foot tall Pine Mountain.

38 Salome Wilderness Area
Size: 18,500 acres (7,487 ha)
Noted for its scenic canyon, which runs nearly the length of the reserve and for its two perennial streams. Trails and access points are limited. Elevations range from 2,600-6,500 feet.

39 Salt River Canyon Wilderness Area
Size: 32,100 (12,990 ha)
A beautiful canyon and the Salt River bisect this rugged wilderness area. Trails are not maintained and most access is via water. Rapids can be dangerous and should be studied before navigating the river. Elevations range from 2,200-4,200 feet.

40 Sierra Ancha Wilderness Area
Size: 20,850 acres (8,438 ha)
Area is noted for its steep box canyons and large mesas. Good trail system winds through the extremely rough terrain. Elevations range from the desert floor to 8,000 feet.

41 Superstition Wilderness Area
Size: 159,750 acres (64,650 ha)
Popular wilderness area receives heavy use and is one of the few areas in Arizona where one can experience blistering summer heat and winter snowstorms. Excellent trail system.

DESERT AWARENESS

Before venturing out on a day hike or a backcountry adventure in the desert, it is important to understand the relative risks and how to deal with emergency situations. Everyone venturing into in the desert should understand the basics of wilderness survival and emergency first aid and avoid travelling alone.

1. Water
- Always carry water, even in winter. A rule of thumb is to allow for one gallon of water per person per day.
- If you are hiking, always turn back once half your water is gone.
- If you are planning a hike of a day or more, it is advisable to cache a store of water somewhere along your trail before setting off. Desert springs are unreliable sources of fresh water and may be contaminated.

You can last three days without water and 30 days without food. It will likely cost you more energy to find food than you will gain. Water collects in cavities of living and dead plants. Check tree stumps and cup-shaped flowers. The barrel cactus of the southern U.S. has a watery sap that can be consumed; cut top off cactus and mash insides into pulp. The pads of the widespread prickly pear are also a source of water/food. Peel and eat insides. Avoid other cacti as they may be poisonous.

Barrel Cactus Prickly-pear Cactus

2. Wildlife
- Do not touch or feed wildlife. They may carry disease or bite.
- Watch where you step. Many snakes are well-camouflaged and can be sluggish in the morning or after eating.
- Watch where you put your hands. Do not put hands in places you can't see into. Turn over rocks and logs with a stick or tool.
- Anything you leave laying around – shoes, towels, packs – is a potential source of cover/shade for desert critters. Shake them out first.

3. Hiking and Camping
- Avoid desert washes. These steep-sloped gulches may seem like smooth pathways until they fill with flash floods of rainwater. Flooding may occur even if a storm is miles in the distance. As a rule you should stay on ridges or high ground.
- Bring adequate clothing. The desert can be surprisingly cold at night, and a drop of 40°F between day and night is common.
- Carry a map and use a compass. People perish in the desert every year from simply getting lost. If lost, seek shelter and stay put.
- Put food away carefully and avoid leaving crumbs about or wiping your hands on your clothing. Keep all litter stored in a sealed bag and pack it out with you. Food is scarce in the desert and the slightest traces will attract visitors.
- To avoid the intense midday heat, travel earlier and later in the day.

Shelter From Heat

- Find or make a shaded area that does not restrict air circulation.
- Avoid sweating at all times; stay out of high winds that will dehydrate you.
- Avoid sitting or leaning on hot surfaces. Sit on clothing or brush, or dig down into soil where it may be cooler.

4. Driving

- Know your destination. There are a number of wilderness areas and refuges that are off limits to vehicles. Trespassers are subject to substantial fines.
- Prepare for the worst. Temperatures in some areas will top 110°F degrees and the desert is no place to be stuck with a disabled vehicle. Carry water, tools, spare tires, transmission and brake fluid, sunscreen, hats and extra clothing to be safe. A cellular phone and food should also be considered.
- If hiking away from your vehicle, park it on high ground so it will be easier to find when you return.
- Take more than one vehicle when traveling to remote areas.

Navigation

1) Stand a stick in the ground (at least 3 ft./90 cm high) and mark the end of the shadow it casts with a twig (a).
2) After 30 minutes mark the new shadow tip (b);
3) A line through (a) and (b) points East-West with the first mark (a) being West. A line from the base of the shadow stick bisecting (a) and (b) points North.

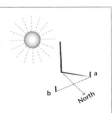

Carry lightweight reference guides that can help you deal with emergency situations.

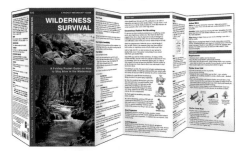

N.B. – The publisher makes no representation or warranties with respect to the accuracy, completeness, correctness or usefulness of this information and specifically disclaims any implied warranties of fitness for a particular purpose. The advice, strategies and/or techniques contained herein may not be suitable for all individuals. The publisher shall not be responsible for any physical harm (up to and including death), loss of profit or other commercial damage. The publisher assumes no liability brought or instituted by individuals or organizations arising out of or relating in any way to the application and/or use of the information, advice and strategies contained herein.

MAMMALS

❏ Abert's Squirrel
❏ American Badger
❏ American Beaver
❏ Arizona Gray Squirrel
❏ Black Bear
❏ Black-tailed Jackrabbit
❏ Bobcat
❏ Botta's Pocket Gopher
❏ Brazilian Free-tailed Bat
❏ Cactus Mouse
❏ Cliff Chipmunk
❏ Coati
❏ Common Porcupine
❏ Common Raccoon
❏ Coyote
❏ Deer Mouse
❏ Desert Bighorn Sheep
❏ Desert Cottontail
❏ Desert Shrew
❏ Eastern Cottontail
❏ Elk
❏ Gray Fox
❏ Gunnison's Prairie Dog
❏ Harris' Antelope Squirrel
❏ Hoary Bat
❏ House Mouse
❏ Javelina
❏ Kit Fox
❏ Mountain Lion
❏ Mule Deer
❏ Muskrat
❏ Norway Rat
❏ Ord's Kangaroo Rat
❏ Pronghorn
❏ Red Squirrel
❏ Ringtail
❏ Rock Squirrel
❏ Round-tailed Ground Squirrel
❏ Striped Skunk
❏ Western Pipistrelle
❏ Western Spotted Skunk
❏ White-tailed Deer
❏ White-throated Woodrat

BIRDS

❏ Acorn Woodpecker
❏ American Coot
❏ American Kestrel
❏ American Robin
❏ American White Pelican
❏ Anna's Hummingbird
❏ Ash-throated Flycatcher
❏ Bald Eagle
❏ Barn Swallow
❏ Belted Kingfisher
❏ Black Phoebe
❏ Black-chinned Hummingbird
❏ Black-throated Sparrow
❏ Brewer's Blackbird
❏ Brown-headed Cowbird
❏ Bullock's Oriole
❏ Cactus Wren
❏ California Condor
❏ Canada Goose
❏ Cattle Egret
❏ Cedar Waxwing
❏ Cinnamon Teal
❏ Common Black Hawk
❏ Common Raven
❏ Curve-billed Thrasher
❏ Dark-eyed Junco
❏ Double-crested Cormorant
❏ Elf Owl
❏ European Starling
❏ Gambel's Quail
❏ Gila Woodpecker
❏ Golden Eagle
❏ Great Blue Heron
❏ Great Egret
❏ Greater Roadrunner
❏ Great Horned Owl
❏ Great-tailed Grackle
❏ Green Heron
❏ Green-winged Teal
❏ Harris's Hawk
❏ Horned Lark
❏ House Finch
❏ House Sparrow
❏ Inca Dove

❏ Killdeer
❏ Lesser Goldfinch
❏ Lesser Nighthawk
❏ Loggerhead Shrike
❏ Mallard
❏ Mountain Chickadee
❏ Mourning Dove
❏ Northern Cardinal
❏ Northern Flicker
❏ Northern Mockingbird
❏ Northern Pintail
❏ Northern Shoveler
❏ Osprey
❏ Phainopepla
❏ Pied-billed Grebe
❏ Purple Martin
❏ Pyrrhuloxia
❏ Red-tailed Hawk
❏ Red-winged Blackbird
❏ Rock Pigeon
❏ Scaled Quail
❏ Scott's Oriole
❏ Song Sparrow
❏ Snowy Egret
❏ Spotted Towhee
❏ Steller's Jay
❏ Turkey Vulture
❏ Verdin
❏ Vermilion Flycatcher
❏ Western Bluebird
❏ Western Meadowlark
❏ Western Scrub-Jay
❏ Western Tanager
❏ White-breasted Nuthatch
❏ White-winged Dove
❏ Wild Turkey
❏ Yellow Warbler
❏ Yellow-headed Blackbird
❏ Yellow-rumped Warbler

REPTILES

❏ Arizona Coral Snake
❏ Arizona (Gilbert's) Skink
❏ Arizona Ridge-nosed
   Rattlesnake
❏ Black-necked Garter Snake
❏ Black-tailed Rattlesnake
❏ Chuckwalla
❏ Collared Lizard
❏ Common Kingsnake
❏ Desert Box Turtle
❏ Desert Iguana
❏ Desert Tortoise
❏ Gila Monster
❏ Glossy Snake
❏ Gopher Snake
❏ Pond Slider
❏ Regal Horned Lizard
❏ Short-horned Lizard
❏ Side-blotched Lizard
❏ Sonoran Mud Turtle
❏ Western Banded Gecko
❏ Western Diamondback
   Rattlesnake
❏ Western Fence Lizard
❏ Western Rattlesnake
❏ Western Whiptail
❏ Zebra-tailed Lizard

AMPHIBIANS

❏ Arizona Treefrog
❏ Bullfrog
❏ Canyon Treefrog
❏ Northern Leopard Frog
❏ Red-spotted Toad
❏ Western Spadefoot Toad

FISHES

❏ Apache Trout
❏ Black Bullhead
❏ Black Crappie
❏ Blue Catfish
❏ Bluegill
❏ Brook Trout
❏ Brown Trout
❏ Channel Catfish
❏ Common Carp
❏ Fathead Minnow
❏ Flathead Catfish

❏ Gila Topminnow
❏ Golden Shiner
❏ Goldfish
❏ Largemouth Bass
❏ Longfin Dace
❏ Mosquitofish
❏ Mozambique Tilapia
❏ Rainbow Trout
❏ Red Shiner
❏ Smallmouth Bass
❏ Speckled Dace
❏ Spikedace
❏ Striped Bass
❏ Walleye
❏ White Crappie
❏ Yellow Perch

INVERTEBRATES

❏ Bark Scorpion
❏ Black Widow Spider
❏ Desert Millipede
❏ Desert Tarantula
❏ Grand Western Cicada
❏ Termites
❏ Tiger Beetle

TREES, SHRUBS & CACTI

❏ Arizona Alder
❏ Arizona Cypress
❏ Arizona Sycamore
❏ Arizona Walnut
❏ Arizona White Oak
❏ Arroyo Willow
❏ Banana Yucca
❏ Barrel Cactus
❏ Beavertail Cactus
❏ Beehive Cactus
❏ Birchleaf Mountain Mahogany
❏ Blue Spruce
❏ Bristlecone Pine
❏ Brittlebrush
❏ Buckhorn Cholla
❏ California Fan Palm

❏ Canary Palm
❏ Catclaw
❏ Century Plant
❏ Cliffrose
❏ Colorado Pinyon Pine
❏ Creosote Bush
❏ Date Palm
❏ Desert Prickly Pear Cactus
❏ Desert Willow
❏ Douglas-Fir
❏ Emory Oak
❏ Engelmann Spruce
❏ Fishhook Cactus
❏ Foothill Palo Verde
❏ Fremont Cottonwood
❏ Gambel Oak
❏ Hedgehog Cactus
❏ Honey Mesquite
❏ Ironwood
❏ Jojoba
❏ Joshua-Tree
❏ Jumping Cholla
❏ Limber Pine
❏ Lombardy Popular
❏ Mohave Yucca
❏ New Mexico Locust
❏ Ocotillo
❏ Organ Pipe Cactus
❏ Ponderosa Pine
❏ Quaking Aspen
❏ Rabbitbrush
❏ Rocky Mountain Juniper
❏ Rocky Mountain Maple
❏ Saguaro
❏ Screwbean Mesquite
❏ Soaptree Yucca
❏ Teddybear Cholla
❏ Utah Juniper
❏ Weeping Willow
❏ White Fir

WILDFLOWERS

White
❏ Arrowhead
❏ Bindweed
❏ Bladder Campion
❏ Common Ice Plant
❏ Cow Parsnip
❏ Desert Ajo Lily
❏ Desert Star
❏ Dune Primrose
❏ English Daisy
❏ Fragrant Waterlily
❏ Phlox
❏ Prickly Poppy
❏ Queen Anne's Lace
❏ Sacred Datura
❏ White Clover
❏ Yarrow

Yellow, Orange & Green
❏ Arizona Mule's Ear
❏ Arizona Poppy
❏ Buffalo Gourd
❏ Butterflyweed
❏ Chinchweed
❏ Common Dandelion
❏ Common Monkey Flower
❏ Common Plantain
❏ Common Sunflower
❏ Creamcups
❏ Desert Marigold
❏ Devil's Claw
❏ Golden Columbine
❏ Goldenrod
❏ Goldfields
❏ Hooker's Evening Primrose
❏ Mexican Goldpoppy
❏ Prince's Plume
❏ Snakeweed
❏ St. John's Wort
❏ Subalpine Buttercup
❏ Tree Tobacco
❏ Woolly Mullein
❏ Yellow Salsify

Red & Pink
❏ Beardtongue
❏ Canada Thistle
❏ Cardinal Flower
❏ Common Fleabane
❏ Desert Four O'Clock
❏ Desert Globemallow
❏ Desert Mariposa Lily
❏ Desert Primrose
❏ Fairy Slipper
❏ Fireweed
❏ Firewheel
❏ Indian Paintbrush
❏ Owl Clover
❏ Pine Drops
❏ Pipsissewa
❏ Shooting Star
❏ Skyrocket
❏ Storksbill
❏ Wild Rose

Blue & Purple
❏ American Vetch
❏ Arizona Lupine
❏ Awl-leaf Aster
❏ Blue Dicks
❏ Blue-eyed Grass
❏ Chicory
❏ Dayflower
❏ Desert Sand Verbena
❏ Fringed Gentian
❏ Harebell
❏ Monkshood
❏ Oyster Plant
❏ Rocky Mountain Iris
❏ Showy Milkweed
❏ Teasel
❏ Wild Blue Flax

Alternate
Spaced singly along the stem.

Anther
The part of the stamen that produces pollen.

Anadromous
Living in saltwater, breeding in freshwater.

Annual
A plant which completes its life cycle in one year.

Anterior
Pertaining to the front end.

Aquatic
Living in water.

Aquifer
Underground chamber or layer of rock that holds water.

Ascending
Rising or curving upward.

Barbel
An organ near the mouth of fish used to taste, touch, or smell.

Berry
A fruit formed from a single ovary which is fleshy or pulpy and contains one or many seeds.

Bloom
A whitish powdery or waxy covering.

Brackish
Water that is part freshwater and part saltwater.

Bract
A modified, often scale-like, leaf, usually small.

Branchlet
A twig from which leaves grow.

Boss
A rounded knob between the eyes of some toads.

Burrow
A tunnel excavated and inhabited by an animal.

Carnivorous
Feeding primarily on meat.

Catkin
A caterpillar-like drooping cluster of small flowers.

Cold-blooded
Refers to animals which are unable to regulate their own body temperature. 'Ectotherm' is the preferred term for this characteristic since many 'cold-blooded' species like reptiles are at times able to maintain a warmer body temperature than that of 'warm-blooded' species like mammals.

Conifer
A cone-bearing tree, usually evergreen.

Coral
The limestone skeletal deposits of coral polyps.

Coverts
Small feathers that cover the underside (undertail) or top (uppertail) of the base of bird's tail.

Deciduous
Shedding leaves annually.

Diurnal
Active primarily during the day.

Dorsal
Pertaining to the back or upper surface.

Ecology
The study of the relationships between organisms, and between organisms and their environment.

Endangered
Species threatened with extinction.

Epiphyte
A plant that obtains nourishment from nutrients in the air and rain. They often live on host plants like trees without harming them.

Endemic
Living only in a particular area.

Flower
Reproductive structure of a plant.

Flower stalk
The stem bearing the flowers.

Fruit
The matured, seed-bearing ovary.

Gamete
An egg or sperm cell.

Habitat
The physical area in which organisms live.

Herbivorous
Feeding primarily on vegetation.

Insectivorous
Feeding primarily on insects.

Introduced
Species brought by humans to an area outside its normal range.

Invertebrate
Animals lacking backbones, e.g., worms, slugs, crustaceans, insects, shellfish.

Larva
Immature forms of an animal which differ from the adult.

Lateral
Located away from the mid-line, at or near the sides.

Lobe
A projecting part of a leaf or flower, usually rounded.

Mesa
High, flat-topped mountain or hill with steeply sloping sides.

Molting
Loss of feathers, hair or skin while renewing plumage, coat or scales.

Morphs
A color variation of a species that is regular and not related to sex, age or season.

Nest
A structure built for shelter or insulation.

Nocturnal
Active primarily at night.

Omnivorous
Feeding on both animal and vegetable food.

Ovary
The female sex organ which is the site of egg production and maturation.

Perennial
A plant that lives for several years.

Petal
The colored outer parts of a flower head.

Phase
Coloration other than typical.

Pistil
The central organ of the flower which develops into a fruit.

Pollen
The tiny grains produced in the anthers which contain the male reproductive cells.

Posterior
Pertaining to the rear.

Sepal
The outer, usually green, leaf-like structures that protect the flower bud and are located at the base of an open flower.

Species
A group of interbreeding organisms which are reproductively isolated from other groups.

Speculum
A brightly colored, iridescent patch on the wings of some birds, especially ducks.

Spur
A pointed projection.

Subspecies
A relatively uniform, distinct portion of a species population.

Terrestrial
Land dwelling.

Threatened
Species not yet endangered but in imminent danger of being so.

Ungulate
An animal that has hooves.

Ventral
Pertaining to the under or lower surface.

Vertebrate
An animal possessing a backbone.

Warm-blooded
An animal which regulates its blood temperature internally. 'Endotherm' is the preferred term for this characteristic.

Whorl
A circle of leaves or flowers about a stem.

Woolly
Bearing long or matted hairs.

BIBLIOGRAPHY

FLORA

Arizona Traveler Guidebooks. *Arizona Wildflowers: A Guide to Common Varieties.* Frederick: Renaissance House, 1989.

Arnberger, Leslie P. and J. Janish. *Flowers of the Southwest Mountains.* Tucson: Southwest Parks and Monuments Association, 1974.

Barnard, Edward S. and Sharon Fass Yates, eds. *Reader's Digest North American Wildlife: Wildflowers.* Pleasantville: Reader's Digest Association, 1998.

Bowers, Janice E. *100 Desert Wildflowers of the Southwest.* Tucson: Southwest Parks and Monuments Association, 1998.

Bowers, Janice E. *Shrubs and Trees of the Southwest Deserts.* Tucson: Western National Parks Association, 1993.

Brockman, C.F. *Trees of North America.* New York: Golden Press, 1979.

Coombes, Allen J. *Eye Witness Handbooks: Trees.* New York: Dorling Kindersley, 1992.

Desert Botanical Garden Staff. *Arizona Highways Present Desert Wildflowers.* Phoenix: Arizona Department of Transportation, 1988.

Dodge, N. and J. Janish. *Flowers of the Southwest Deserts.* Tucson: Southwest Parks and Monuments Association, 1985.

Earle, W. Hubert. *Cacti of the Southwest.* Phoenix: Desert Botanical Garden, 1980.

Easy Field Guide to Common Desert Cactus of Arizona. Phoenix: Primer Publishers, 1985.

Elias, Thomas S. *The Complete Trees of North America: Field Guide and Natural History.* New York: Van Nostrand Reinhold, 1980.

Elmore, F.H. *Shrubs and Trees of Southwest Uplands.* Tucson: Southwest Parks and Monuments Association, 1981.

Epple, A.O. *Plants of Arizona.* Helena: Falcon Press, 1995.

Fischer, Pierre C. *70 Common Cacti of the Southwest.* Tucson: Southwest Parks and Monuments Association, 1989.

Heil, K.D. *Familiar Cacti of North America.* New York: Alfred A. Knopf, 1993.

Lanzara, Paoloa and Mariella Pizzetti. *Simon & Schuster's Guide to Trees.* New York: Simon & Schuster, 1978.

Little, Elbert L. *National Audubon Society Field Guide to North American Trees: Western Region.* New York: Alfred A. Knopf, 1980.

Magley, Beverley. *Arizona Wildflowers: A Children's Field Guide to the State's Most Common Flowers.* Helena: Falcon Press, 1991.

Mielke, Judy. *Native Plants for Southwestern Landscapes.* Austin: University of Texas Press, 1993.

Nelson, Richard and Sharon Nelson. *Easy Field Guide to Common Trees of Arizona.* Phoenix: Primer Publishers, 1994.

Niehaus, Theodore F., et al. *Southwestern and Texas Wildflowers.* Boston: Houghton Mifflin, 1984.

Orth Epple, Anne. *A Field Guide to the Plants of Arizona.* Helena: Falcon Press, 1997.

Quinn, Meg. *Wildflowers of the Desert Southwest.* Tucson: Rio Nuevo Publishers, 2000.

Spellenberg, R. *The Audubon Society Field Guide to North American Wildflowers – Western Region.* New York: Alfred A. Knopf, 1979.

Venning, D. *Wildflowers of North America.* New York: Golden Press, 1984.

MAMMALS

Boitani, Luigi and Stefania Bartoli. *Simon & Schuster's Guide to Mammals.* New York: Simon & Schuster, 1983.

Bureau of Land Management Yuma Field Office. *Mammals of the Yuma Field Office.* Yuma: Bureau of Land Management, nd.

Burt, William Henry. *A Field Guide to the Mammals: Field Marks of All North American Species Found North of Mexico.* 3rd ed. Boston: Houghton Mifflin, 1976.

Cockrum, E. Lendell. *Mammals of the Southwest.* Tucson: The University of Arizona Press, 1982.

Halfpenny, J.C. *A Field Guide to Mammal Tracking in North America.* Boulder: Johnson Books, 1986.

Hoffmeister, Donald, F. *Mammals of Arizona.* Tucson: University of Arizona Press, 1986.

Hoffmeister, Donald F. *Mammals of Grand Canyon.* Urbana: University of Illinois Press, 1971.

Mays, Buddy. *Guide to Western Wildlife.* Rev. 3rd ed. San Francisco: Chronicle Books, 1988.

Murie, Olaus J. *A Field Guide to Animal Tracks.* 2nd ed. Boston: Houghton Mifflin, 1982.

Nelson, Richard and Sharon Nelson. *Easy Field Guide to Common Desert Mammals of Arizona.* Phoenix: Primer Publishers, 1985.

Olin, G. and D. Thompson. *Mammals of Southwestern Deserts.* Tucson: Southwest Parks and Monuments Association, 1982.

United States Department of Agriculture. *Mammals of the Tonto National Forest: A Checklist.* Forest Service, 1998.

Walker, Ernest P., et al. *Mammals of the World.* 2 vols. Baltimore: Johns Hopkins Press, 1965.

Whitaker, John O., Jr. *National Audubon Society Field Guide to North American Mammals.* Rev. ed. New York: Alfred A. Knopf, 1996.

BIRDS

Alsop, Fred J., III. *Smithsonian Handbooks Birds of North America: Western Region.* New York: Dorling Kindersley, 2001.

Ayer, Eleanor. *Arizona Traveller – Birds of Arizona.* Washington, D.C.: RH Publications, 1988.

Barnard, Edward S. and Sharon Fass Yates, eds. *Reader's Digest North American Wildlife: Birds.* Pleasantville: Reader's Digest Association, 1998.

Bureau of Land Management Yuma Field Office. *Birds of the Yuma Field Office.* Yuma: Bureau of Land Management, nd.

Cunningham, Richard. *50 Common Birds of the Southwest.* Tucson: Southwest Parks and Monuments Association, 1992.

Davis, Barbara L. *A Field Guide to Birds of the Desert Southwest.* Houston: Gulf Publishing Company, 1997.

Davis, W.A. and S.M. Russel. *Birds in Southeastern Arizona.* Tucson: Tucson Audubon Society, 1984.

Latimer, Jonathan P., et al. *Birds of North America: A Guide to Field Identification.* Rev. and updated. New York: St. Martin's Press, 2001.

McMillon, Bill. *Birding Arizona: 45 Premier Birding Locations.* Helena: Falcon Press, 1995.

National Geographic Field Guide to the Birds of North America. 4th ed. Washington, D.C.: National Geographic Society, 1987.

Nelson, Richard and Sharon Nelson. *Easy Field Guide to Common Desert Birds of Arizona.* Phoenix: Primer Publishers, 1991.

Peterson, Roger Tory. *A Field Guide to Western Birds.* 3rd ed. Boston: Houghton Mifflin, 1990.

Phillips, A., Marshall J. and Monson, G. *The Birds of Arizona.* Tucson: University of Arizona, 1964.

Robbins, Chandler L., et al. *Birds of North America.* New York: Golden Press, 1988.

Sibley, David Allen. *The Sibley Guide to Birds.* New York: Alfred A. Knopf, 2000.

Southeastern Arizona Birding Trail. Bureau of Land Management Arizona State Field Office, nd.

Tekiela, Stan. *Birds of Arizona Field Guide.* Cambridge: Adventure Publications, 2003.

Udvardy, Miklos D.F. *The Audubon Society Field Guide to North American Birds: Western Region.* New York: Alfred A. Knopf, 1994.

Witzeman, Janet Lauster, et al. *Birds of Phoenix and Maricopa County, Arizona.* Phoenix: Maricopa Audubon Society, 1997.

REPTILES & AMPHIBIANS

Behler, John .L. *The Audubon Society Field Guide to North American Reptiles and Amphibians.* New York: Alfred A. Knopf, 1979.

Behler, John L. *National Audubon Society Pocket Guide: Familiar Reptiles and Amphibians of North America.* New York: Alfred A. Knopf, 1995.

Bureau of Land Management Yuma Field Office. *Amphibians and Reptiles of the Yuma Field Office.* Yuma: Bureau of Land Management, nd.

Capula, Massimo. *Simon & Schuster's Guide to Reptiles and Amphibians of the World.* New York: Simon & Schuster, 1989.

BIBLIOGRAPHY

Discovery Channel Reptiles and Amphibians. New York: Discovery Books, 2000.

Hanson, Jonathan and Roseann Beggy Hanson. *50 Common Reptiles and Amphibians of the Southwest.* Tucson: Southwest Parks and Monuments Association, 1997.

Kirshner, David S. *My First Pocket Guide: Reptiles and Amphibians.* Washington, D.C.: National Geographic Society, 2001.

Nelson, Richard C. and Sharon Nelson. *Easy Field Guide to Common Snakes of Arizona.* Glenwood: Tecolote Press, 1977.

Smith, Hobart M. and Edmund D. Brodie, Jr. *Reptiles of North America: A Guide to Field Identification.* New York: St. Martin's Press, 1982.

Smith, Robert L. *Venomous Animals of Arizona.* Tucson: University of Arizona Press, 1982.

Stebbins, Robert C. *A Field Guide to Western Reptiles and Amphibians.* 2nd ed. Boston: Houghton Mifflin, 1985.

Ubertazzi Tanara, Milli. *The World of Amphibians and Reptiles.* Berkshire: Sampson Low, 1978.

United States Department of Agriculture. *Amphibians and Reptiles of the Tonto National Forest: A Checklist.* Forest Service, 2004.

Zim, Herbert S. and Hobart M. Smith. *Reptiles and Amphibians.* Rev. ed. New York: Golden Press, 1987.

FISHES

Boschung, Herbert T. Jr., et al. *The Audubon Society Field Guide to North American Fishes, Whales and Dolphins.* New York: Alfred Knopf, 1989.

Gilbert, Carter R. and James D. Williams. *National Audubon Society Field Guide to Fishes: North America.* Rev. ed. New York: Alfred A. Knopf, 2002.

Page, Lawrence and Brooks M. Burr. *A Field Guide to Freshwater Fishes: North America North of Mexico.* Boston: Houghton Mifflin, 1991.

United States Department of Agriculture. *Fishes of the Tonto National Forest: A Checklist.* Forest Service, 2004.

INSECTS

Arnett, Ross H. Jr. and Richard L. Jacques, Jr. *Simon & Schuster's Guide to Insects.* New York: Simon & Schuster, 1981.

Borror, Donald J. and Richard E. White. *A Field Guide to Insects: America North of Mexico.* Boston: Houghton Mifflin, 1970.

Carter, David. *Eyewitness Handbooks: Butterflies and Moths.* New York: Dorling Kindersley, 1992.

Farrand, John, Jr., ed. *National Audubon Society Pocket Guide: Insects and Spiders.* New York: Alfred A. Knopf, 1995.

Forey, Pamela and Cecilia Fitzsimons. *An Instant Guide to Insects.* New York: Gramercy Books, 1999.

Leahy, Christopher. *Peterson First Guide to Insects of North America.* Boston: Houghton Mifflin, 1987.

Levi, Herbert W. and Lorna R. Levi. *Spiders and Their Kin.* New York: St. Martin's Press, 1996.

McGavin, George C. *Insects: Spiders and Other Terrestrial Arthropods.* New York: Dorling Kindersley, 2000.

Milne, Lorus and Margery Milne. *National Audubon Society Field Guide to North American Insects and Spiders.* New York: Alfred A. Knopf, 2000.

Mitchell, Robert T. and Herbert S. Zim. *Butterflies and Moths: A Guide to the More Common American Species.* New York: St. Martin's Press, 1992.

Nelson, Richard and Sharon Nelson. *Easy Field Guide to Common Desert Insects.* Phoenix: Primer Publishers, 1996.

Zim, Herbert S. and Clarence Cottam. *Insects: A Guide to Familiar American Insects.* New York: St. Martin's Press, 2001.

NATURAL HISTORY

Aitchison, Stewart. *A Naturalist's Guide to Hiking the Grand Canyon.* New York: Prentice Hall, 1985.

Alcock, John. *Sonoran Desert Spring.* Chicago: University of Chicago Press, 1985.

Alcock, John. *Sonoran Desert Summer.* Tucson: University of Arizona Press, 1990.

Alden, Peter, et al. *National Audubon Society Field Guide to the Southwestern States.* New York: Alfred A. Knopf, 1999.

Arizona Traveler Guidebooks. *Discover Arizona: The Grand Canyon State.* Frederick: Renaissance House, 1988.

Benyus, Janine M. *The Field Guide to Wildlife Habitats of the Western United States.* New York: Simon & Schuster, 1989.

Bureau of Land Management Safford Field Office. *Hot Well Dunes Recreation Area.* Safford: Bureau of Land Management, nd.

Chronic, Halka. *Roadside Geology of Arizona.* Missoula: Mountain Press Publishing, 1983.

Krutch, Joseph Wood. *The Desert Year.* New York: Viking Press, 1964.

Larson, Peggy and Lane Larson. *A Sierra Club Naturalist's Guide to the Deserts of the Southwest.* San Francisco: Sierra Club Books, 1977.

Lowe, Charles H. *Arizona's Natural Environment – Landscapes and Habitats.* Tucson: University of Arizona Press, 1972.

MacMahon, James A. *Deserts.* New York: Alfred A. Knopf, 1987.

McNab, W. Henry and Peter E. Avers. *Ecological Subregions of the United States: Section Descriptions.* Washington, D.C.: United States Department of Agriculture, 1994.

McQueen, Jane B, ed. *The Complete Guide to America's National Parks.* 1994-1995 ed. Washington, D.C.: National Park Foundation, 1995.

Perry, John and Jane G. Perry. *The Sierra Club Guide to the Natural Areas of New Mexico, Arizona and Nevada.* San Francisco, CA: Sierra Club Books, 1985.

Phillips, Steven J. and Patricia W. Comus, eds. *A Natural History of the Sonoran Desert.* Tucson: Arizona-Sonora Desert Museum Press, 2000.

Ransom, Jay Ellis. *Harper & Row's Complete Field Guide to North American Wildlife.* Western ed. New York: Harper & Row, 1981.

Riley, Laura and William Riley. *Guide to the National Wildlife Refuges.* New York: Collier Books, 1992.

Snyder, Ernest E. *Arizona Outdoor Guide.* Golden West Publishers, Longview, AZ, 1985.

Tweit, Susan J. *The Great Southwest Nature Factbook.* Anchorage: Alaska Northwest Books, 1992.

Warren, Scott S. *Exploring Arizona's Wild Areas: A Guide for Hikers, Backpackers, Climbers, X-C Skiers, & Paddlers.* Seattle: The Mountaineers, 1999.

Welles, Philip. *Meet the Southwest Deserts.* Rev. 2nd ed. Tucson: Dale Stuart King, 1973.

Wernert, Susan J., ed. *Reader's Digest North American Wildlife.* Pleasantville: Reader's Digest Association, 1982.

Whitney, Stephen. *A Field Guide to the Grand Canyon.* New York: Quill, 1982.

Waterford Press Series

Waterford Press produces reference guides that introduce novices to nature, science and adventure. Laminated for durability, these handy folding guides are a great source of portable information, ready to take anywhere, anytime!

POCKET NATURALIST® GUIDES

These simplified guides introduce novices to nature and natural phenomena. Ideal for field use, each pocket-sized, folding guide to plants and animals highlights up to 150 species. The nature series includes three guides to every state, the nation's most prominent national parks and the world's top eco-tourism destinations. Laminated for durability, they are the ideal field references for residents and tourists alike.

DURAGUIDE™

Duraguide® is Waterford's line of durable folding reference guides to outdoor activities including boating, fishing, camping, animal tracking, etc. These guides are built to last, weigh only one ounce, and are ideal for field use by novices and experts alike.

PATHFINDER OUTDOOR SURVIVAL GUIDES™

Co-authored by master woodsman and wilderness survival expert Dave Canterbury, this series of 10 guides reflects his common sense approach to survivability he teaches in his survival school programs.

ADVENTURE SET SERIES

The Waterford Press/National Geographic Maps Adventure Sets consist of a Pocket Naturalist® Guide and National Geographic map, ideal, lightweight references to take hiking or driving while exploring the world's most spectacular places.

DISASTER SURVIVAL GUIDES™

Natural disasters have been increasing in recent years, resulting in catastrophic damages worldwide. Based on international disaster protocols, each guide provides instructions on what to do before, during and after a natural disaster to protect themselves and their property. Also included in each guide are smartphone QR codes that link to the websites of various emergency services agencies.

FIELD GUIDES

These beautifully illustrated field guides highlight over 300 of the familiar species of plants and animals in some of the nation's most ecologically diverse states. Each guide also includes information on geography, climate, ecosystems and over 100 of the top natural attractions in each state.

NATURE ACTIVITY BOOKS

Designed to complement the school curricula of grades K-2 and 3-5, our Nature Activity Books features a variety of creative activities and games – word searches, crosswords, quizzes, origami, mazes, puzzles and drawing/coloring activities – to encourage interest and engage children in nature and the natural sciences.

Over 650 titles with more than 5 million sold!

**For a catalog, or to order, call 800-434-2555
or visit our website at www.waterfordpress.com**

Scan this code to view the entire product line.